THE FIRST-YEAR EXPERIENCE
MONOGRAPH SERIES NO. 26

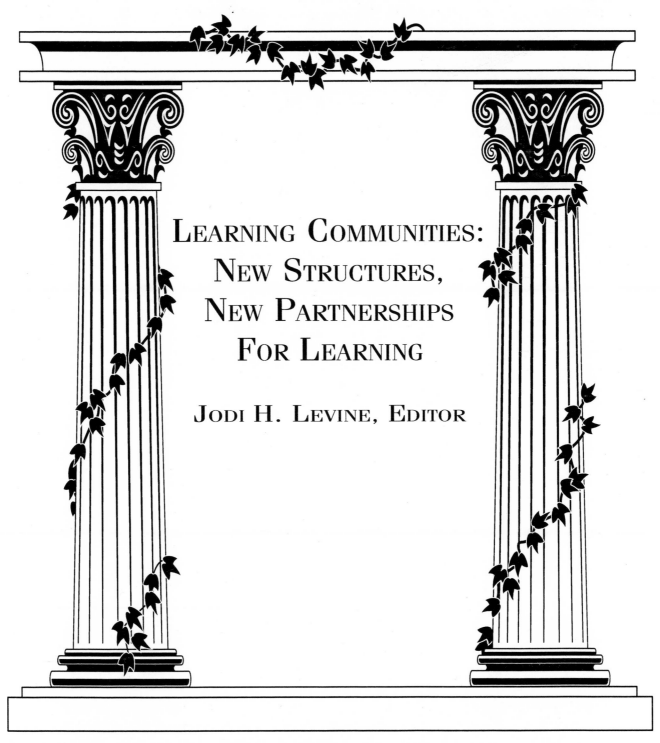

LEARNING COMMUNITIES: NEW STRUCTURES, NEW PARTNERSHIPS FOR LEARNING

JODI H. LEVINE, EDITOR

NATIONAL RESOURCE CENTER FOR THE FIRST-YEAR EXPERIENCE AND STUDENTS IN TRANSITION
UNIVERSITY OF SOUTH CAROLINA, 1999

Cite as:

Levine, J. H. (Ed.). (1999). *Learning communities: New structures, new partnerships for learning* (Monograph No. 26). Columbia, SC: University of South Carolina, National Resource Center for The First-Year Experience and Students in Transition.

Sample chapter citation:

Elliott, J. L., & Decker, E. (1999). Garnering the fundamental resources for learning communities. In J. H. Levine (Ed.), *Learning communities: New structures, new partnerships for learning* (Monograph No. 26) (pp. 19-28). Columbia, SC: University of South Carolina, National Resource Center for The First-Year Experience and Students in Transition.

Additional copies of this monograph may be ordered at $30 each from the National Resource Center for The First-Year Experience and Students in Transition, University of South Carolina, 1629 Pendleton Street, Columbia, SC 29208. Telephone (803) 777-6029. Telefax (803) 777-4699.

Special gratitude is expressed to Tracy L. Skipper, Assistant Editor, for editing, design, and layout of this book; to Dr. Betsy O. Barefoot, Co-Director for Publications and Research; and to Dr. Dorothy S. Fidler, Senior Managing Editor.

ISBN Number: 1-889271-27-6

TABLE OF CONTENTS

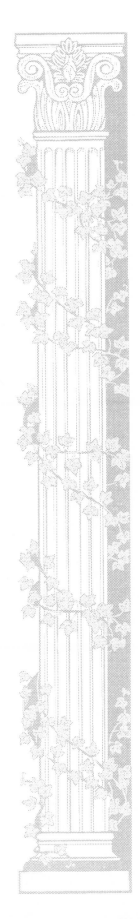

FOREWORD

John N. Gardner

If I were to be asked what structural and pedagogical innovation currently being developed in American higher education may hold the greatest promise for improving first-year student academic performance and retention, I can now argue that it may well be the learning community! That is about as high a form of tribute as I can pay in an introductory statement on any topic.

My colleagues and I at the National Resource Center for The First-Year Experience and Students in Transition have, over the past decade, followed with great respect the work of our colleagues around the country in developing this pioneering intervention. We are especially indebted to educators in Oregon and Washington and to the leaders of the Washington Center for Undergraduate Education for calling this extraordinarily promising concept to our attention.

The basic purpose of the National Center is to provide information to college and university educators (faculty, academic administrators, and student personnel officers) to improve the learning, success, satisfaction, retention, and graduation rates of first-year college students. We would be doing a disservice to educators if we did not have information available on learning communities and first-year students. Until this monograph appeared in print, we did not have such information. Thus, I am now delighted to be able to rectify that significant deficit.

As is likely the case for many readers of this monograph, I have only recently attempted to develop a learning community pilot on my own campus. I can now say that I have personally experienced a number of the trials, tribulations, and rewards described in this monograph. My own campus, though, still has much, much further to go; I am hoping that this monograph will inform colleagues here and around the country about ways to pilot and ultimately institutionalize this promising concept.

The topic of learning communities also has a great appeal to me because it involves several of the core assumptions which have grounded the work of the National Center; for example, the notion that a partnership between faculty, academic administrators, and student affairs administrators is central to the success of learning communities. Similarly, intentional faculty/staff development is indispensable to the success of learning communities. Also the educational intervention nearest and dearest to my own heart, the first-year seminar, plays a central role in integrating many learning communities.

As an illustration of collaboration, this monograph would not have been possible without a partnership developed between the many contributors to this work. We are especially indebted to Dr. Jodi Levine of Temple University who is the epitome of a pioneering crusader for launching and institutionalizing learning communities. Her vision for this monograph and her extraordinary competence and energy made this project a reality.

Before reading this entire manuscript, I thought that I was reasonably informed on this topic. But this monograph has increased my own intellectual understanding and appreciation of learning communities. I am optimistic that this monograph will help many of our readers find both the courage and the information necessary to initiate their own versions of learning communities. There are so many models, so many possibilities, that I am sure this piece will stimulate your imagination, and more importantly, your action. In the future if a need for a second edition arises, we sincerely solicit your experiences and recommendations to further strengthen this publication for the next generation of learning community pioneers.

John N. Gardner
University of South Carolina
January, 1999

INTRODUCTION

Jodi H. Levine, Editor

In 1993, a colleague came to me with news that our institution, Temple University, had just received a significant grant to implement learning communities across our general studies curriculum. I was an academic advisor and a doctoral student at the time; she asked me to begin researching the concept of learning communities to facilitate our planning. Little did I know that a year later I would join our new learning community program as its coordinator.

A literature search led me to Gabelnick, MacGregor, Matthews, and Smith (1990), a monograph entitled *Learning Communities: Creating Connections Among Students, Faculty, and Disciplines*. Their work explained the theoretical and historical principles on which learning communities are based and offered a definition and overview of the elements needed to build effective learning community programs.

Information drawn from the literature helped shape Temple's learning community program; but at the beginning, conversations with other people involved in learning community work were the most helpful. I quickly realized that definitions and commonly used approaches to learning communities were only templates on which we could base our model. The learning communities at our university would need to reflect the teaching, learning, and organizational culture of our campus. There was still, however, a great deal to be learned by collecting "recipes for success" from other programs.

When John N. Gardner and his colleagues at the National Resource Center for The First-Year Experience and Students in Transition invited me to serve as editor-in-chief for a monograph on learning communities and the first-year experience, I saw an opportunity to address the connections between programs for learning communities, students in transition, and faculty development while offering suggestions for facilitating the design and implementation of such programs across many types of institutions. My goal was to develop a monograph that combined theory with examples of good practice and recommendations for building and sustaining effective learning communities.

How is the term "learning communities" used in this monograph? There was never an attempt to get these authors to agree on a common definition. The very nature of learning communities—adaptability and flexibility—make an ultimate definition an elusive goal. The first two chapters intentionally discuss definitions and models of learning communities. Subsequent chapters focus on elements of the work, including the resources needed to build, evaluate, and assess learning communities. The authors describe challenges unique to learning communities and often offer the experiences on their campuses as examples. The definitions on which they rely are reflected in the work they do with their respective programs.

Individually, each chapter provides insight into components of learning communities. Taken collectively, the chapters deepen the reader's understanding of the characteristics of effective learning community programs. What are the elements shared by the learning communities described in this monograph? First, learning communities involve the intentional restructuring of curriculum to bring faculty, students, student affairs professionals, and academic administrators together to share common learning experiences. Second, the planning, building, and maintaining of a learning community will require cross-campus partnerships and conversations regarding intended outcomes. Finally, all involved in the effort need to recognize that learning communities challenge traditional models of teaching and learning.

This monograph also addresses questions that veteran and novice learning community practitioners typically confront. Why do we establish learning communities? How can the undergraduate curriculum be redesigned or structured to incorporate learning communities? Are learning communities an effective way to structure the freshman year experience? What does it take to build and sustain effective learning community programs? How do we establish the cross-campus partnerships essential to the work? How do we know our learning communities are achieving their intended outcomes?

The individuals who contributed to this mono-

graph are practitioners in the field who know how to build learning community programs. All have engaged in the work. In preparing their chapters, the authors were asked not only to draw upon the literature and research that influenced their individual programs, but also to reflect on the lessons they learned along the way. What were their successes and their disappointments, and how did they overcome challenges?

In Chapter 1, Anne Goodsell Love defines the characteristics of learning communities and provides a historical overview of the educational innovations that influenced the learning community movement. In Chapter 2, Goodsell Love and co-author Kenneth A. Tokuno describe models and dimensions of learning communities. Next, Jeanine L. Elliot and Emily Decker discuss the resources needed to build and sustain learning communities.

In Chapter 4, Michaelann M. Jundt, Kenneth K. Etzkorn, and Jason N. Johnson present the logistics of scheduling learning communities, recruiting and registering students. The next two chapters address faculty roles. In Chapter 5, Diane W. Strommer examines faculty perspectives on teaching and learning in learning communities. In Chapter 6, Scott E. Evenbeck, Barbara Jackson, and John McGrew discuss the goals and outcomes of faculty development.

Charles C. Schroeder, Theodore A. Tarkow, and Frankie D. Minor, the authors of Chapter 7, describe opportunities for collaboration between professionals in academic and student affairs in creating learning communities. Continuing the theme of cross-campus collaboration, Jack W. Bennett then discusses the role of academic advisors. In Chapter 9, John N. Gardner, Betsy O. Barefoot, Dorothy S. Fidler, Philip S. Moore, and Melissa Roberts describe uses of the freshman seminar in learning community models. Next, Valerie A. Bystrom considers uses of learning communities at community colleges.

In Chapter 11, Kathi A. Ketcheson and I discuss approaches to evaluating and assessing learning communities. John N. Gardner and I conclude with an examination of the issues raised by this monograph, including a discussion of the implications for the future.

Many people were involved in the writing and editing of this monograph. I would like to offer special thanks to John N. Gardner for recognizing the need for this text and for giving me the opportunity to lead the project and to Betsy O. Barefoot, Dorothy S. Fidler, and publications assistant Tracy L. Skipper for their editing expertise and guidance. I am also grateful to my colleagues and fellow authors, who made my work easier by developing drafts and final versions of their chapters that needed little editing. I continue to learn from the noteworthy work the authors report from their campuses.

All of us involved in the development, writing, and editing of this monograph hope it will become a guide to good practice. Designed to challenge educators, hopefully this monograph will expand the discussion of ways that learning communities can support entering students in their academic and social transition to college.

Reference

Gabelnick, F., MacGregor, J., Matthews, R. S., & Smith, B. L. (Eds.). (1990). Learning communities: Creating connections among students, faculty, and disciplines. *New Directions for Teaching and Learning, 41.* San Francisco: Jossey-Bass.

CHAPTER ONE

What Are Learning Communities?

Anne Goodsell Love

In recent years, there has been an explosion in the use of the term "learning community." A leading computer company sent out a brochure with the headline, "What is the new learning community?" Some educators would suggest that any classroom is a learning community, while others protest that "just linking courses" does not constitute a learning community. These latter educators challenge us to articulate and document the distinctive qualities of learning communities, thereby taking them beyond the popular, buzzword, "stage of development." At any rate, it is safe to say that the appeal of the term "learning community" has taken hold in higher education. But what does it mean within the context of this monograph and within higher education?

The most common understanding of the term, at least among those in higher education in the late 1980s and the 1990s, is that a learning community

> center(s) on a vision of faculty and students—and sometimes administrators, staff and the larger community—working collaboratively toward shared, significant academic goals in environments in which competition, if not absent, is at least de-emphasized. In a learning community, both faculty and students have the opportunity and the responsibility to learn from and help teach each other. (University of Miami, 1998)

Contemporary leaders in the learning communities movement include the faculty and staff at The Evergreen State College in Olympia, Washington; the Washington Center to Improve the Quality of Undergraduate Education; and Collaboration in Undergraduate Education, an "action community" of the American Association for Higher Education, composed of administrators and faculty who have an interest in increasing the use of collaborative learning strategies in higher education. The monograph, *Learning Communities: Creating Connections Among Students, Faculty, and Disciplines* (Gabelnick, MacGregor, Matthews, & Smith, 1990) is still a valuable resource for anyone interested in researching or implementing learning communities. The authors describe learning communities this way:

Learning communities, as we define them, purposefully restructure the curriculum to link together courses or course work so that students find greater coherence in what they are learning as well as increased intellectual interaction with faculty and fellow students. ... learning communities are also usually associated with collaborative and active approaches to learning, some form of team teaching, and interdisciplinary themes. (Gabelnick et al., 1990, p. 5)

Although learning communities can take the form of a few basic models (as discussed in Chapter 2), many variations have evolved to meet the unique needs of diverse student populations and/or the needs of different types of colleges and universities. Therefore, it is difficult to arrive at a common, all-inclusive definition. Whipple's (1987) descriptions of the characteristics of collaboration may provide a useful guide. By outlining the common characteristics of learning communities, we arrive at an understanding of them that is most useful for practitioners and theorists alike.

What are Learning Communities?

Learning communities provide an opportunity to integrate courses in an interdisciplinary manner.

Many learning communities center class readings and assignments around a theme that encourages complementary approaches from a number of disciplinary perspectives. In this way, learning communities become a means of addressing problems of fragmentation in the curriculum or the seeming incoherence of a set of general education requirements. Students often fail to see the relevance of general education courses to their degree programs and their lives after college. Linking courses in ecology, economics, and composition, for example, can set the stage for conversations that overlap the formal course boundaries and provide real-life examples with which all the students are familiar. Courses within learning communities cease to be discrete fragments of a college curriculum. Instead, as courses begin to have some relation to one another, students are also able

to make connections to other facets of their educational experience.

Learning communities help students form social networks among their peers.

Research on first-year student experiences reveals that college classrooms, although full of people, can feel very solitary. Faculty members who teach large lecture classes are familiar with the typical lack of interaction that goes on among students, and students themselves report that "when class begins, you don't talk [to anyone]" (Goodsell, 1993). The research on learning communities suggests that, at least for traditional-age students, social integration to the collegiate environment may be a necessary precursor to academic integration. Especially for first-year students, some amount of comfort with the social arena of a classroom is needed before students are able to risk the admission of ignorance that is necessary for learning to take place. The collaborative nature of learning communities, therefore, encourages students to become integrated both socially and academically at the same time. Students are not asked to sacrifice one at the expense of the other.

Learning communities increase student involvement.

Involvement in learning begins with going to class, but many students choose not to attend their classes. For today's student, class attendance is just one of many competing obligations; so how can attendance be encouraged? Students in learning communities report that they are less likely to miss classes because other people—faculty *and* their peers—will notice if they are not there. Students who move from class to class in a cohort encourage each other not to skip classes and inquire about each other if someone is gone. The expectation of class attendance is not necessarily generated by the faculty member, but by the peer group members who may be dependent on each other for class assignments or out-of-class study groups.

Furthermore, students report that they are more likely to participate in a class where they know one another, and feel more comfortable raising a question or offering an idea. Student involvement measured in hours per week spent studying, use of the library, interaction with faculty, and the amount and type of writing activity increases as well (Tinto, 1997).

Learning communities improve student performance.

Many studies at a variety of colleges and universities have compared the performance of students enrolled in learning communities with their peers who were not. Most studies show modest differences between groups, with students participating in learning communities earning higher GPAs than students who were not in learning communities. Some studies report significant differences in this regard (MacGregor, 1991; Tinto, 1997; Tinto & Goodsell, 1993). Student intellectual development also has been found to increase for students in learning communities as compared to students who were not in learning communities. Using the Measures of Intellectual Development (MID) instrument based on Perry's (1968) scheme of intellectual development, researchers found that students involved in coordinated studies programs "generally made a significant and unusual leap in intellectual development during their learning community experience" (MacGregor, 1991, p. 7). Students entered the programs at dualistic levels of reasoning but exited the programs as early multiplists, meaning that they were more able to see issues from multiple perspectives than when they began, and that they were less likely to expect simple right or wrong answers to questions. This change in the nature of their thinking, in addition to an increase in amount of knowledge gained, makes learning communities a particularly exciting and powerful educational innovation.

Learning communities impact student retention.

Similar to the results of studies on student performance, studies of student retention indicate moderate to large differences in rates of retention, with students in learning communities persisting at

> The overall pattern of the research to date indicates that learning communities assist underprepared students to persist at rates equal to their more prepared peers . . .

greater rates than students who were not in learning communities (MacGregor, 1991). For example, one study found that 83.8% of students in a coordinated studies program persisted to the next semester compared to 80.9% of students in comparison classes; those rates after one year were 66.7% and 52.0%, respectively—a significant difference (Tinto, 1997). Even when retention rates are not significantly different between those students participating in learning communities and those who are not, there is reason to believe that learning communities have a positive impact on student retention. In one study, students who entered college and were placed into developmental courses taught as a learning community did not show a greater rate of retention than non-learning community students; however, a retention rate for developmental studies students comparable to that of students taking non-developmental courses is very encouraging (Tinto & Goodsell Love, 1995). The overall pattern of the research to date indicates that learning communities assist underprepared students to persist at rates equal to their more prepared peers, while regularly admitted students in learning communities persist at higher rates than their peers.

Learning communities provide opportunities for faculty development.

Faculty who teach in learning communities are enthusiastic about the experience, citing the novelty of a sustained conversation with colleagues about teaching and a common group of students to whom they can refer (Gabelnick et al., 1990). Faculty support one another in attempts to try different methods of teaching, such as collaborative learning strategies, and in constructing assignments that cross traditional disciplinary boundaries. Some rediscover the pleasure of being a learner when they are called upon to make connections with topics across courses or read a common text through a different disciplinary lens. Faculty also benefit from the increased social integration of students in learning communities. That students are more likely to attend and participate in class is a welcome change for faculty who have become numbed by students who seem indifferent to what happens in class. It is exciting for faculty to see students engaged by the learning process.

Learning communities shift the focus to student learning outcomes.

Before faculty can decide what to teach, they need to agree on their goals for students. This discussion of goals often leads to an examination of the ways that the goals can be achieved (what teaching methods will be used?) and the ways that the goals can be evaluated or measured (what means of assessment will be used?). If these questions are asked with a willingness to face the answers—and the fact that the answers may require a significant change in teaching practice—then the potential power of learning communities is revealed. A dynamic chain of events is set in motion: A focus on student learning outcomes directs the need for continued faculty development, which in turn facilitates the creation of an arena that promotes effective student learning. Although learning communities may be appealing to administrators because of their potential to increase student retention, the key to retention is increased student learning. No meaningful reform of higher education is likely without addressing questions of what, how, and how much students are learning.

Learning communities allow educators to rethink the ways by which students are taught.

A counseling phrase goes something like this: Comfort the challenged and challenge the comfortable. The same could be said of effective education—that those who are comfortable with their knowledge base need to be challenged to go further, and that those who are feeling challenged by new ideas need to be supported in their struggle to learn. Faculty in learning communities can provide a consistent message about course structure to students, and students can support each other by forming study groups and by sharing common classroom experiences and strategies for success. At the same time, an interdisciplinary approach can unsettle students

by offering no one right answer to a question but many varying answers, depending on the point of view of the respondent. First-year students, typically at dualistic stages of cognitive development, need to be exposed to alternate points of view in order to move them toward multiplistic and relativistic ways of thinking (Perry, 1968). Critical thinking skills frequently are cited as learning outcomes for college students, but often are not modeled in the classroom or intentionally taught. Learning communities are well-positioned to both challenge and support students, thereby enhancing students' abilities to think critically.

Learning communities can become a lens through which the experiences of students at a particular college can be understood.

Designing and implementing a learning commu-nity can be fraught with difficulties (as will be outlined in subsequent chapters), but these same difficulties can highlight obstacles students face every day, such as cumbersome registration policies, or the impact of financial aid on student decisions. Smoothing the way for students to enroll in learning communities may point to ways to improve the registration process overall. Or, in the process of selecting courses for a learning community, faculty and advisors may learn important insights about each other's practices. In addition, an evaluation of the learning community program may reveal strengths and weaknesses beyond the scope of the program. Although this lens-like function of learning communities alone does not merit the adoption of a program, it can be an important side effect that contributes to improvement of other elements of a university or college.

Educational Innovations Influencing Learning Communities

This introductory chapter on learning communities would be incomplete without reference to the strands of educational thought that have influenced the movement, or to some key innovators who have contributed to its development. The monograph by Gabelnick et al. (1990) contains similar historical references, tracing the "roots" of the learning community movement but also paying particular attention to the roots of collaborative learning strategies.

Gabelnick et al. (1990) discuss the contributions of educators most often associated with the development of learning communities: John Dewey, Alexander Meiklejohn, and Joseph Tussman. In the 1920s, Dewey and Meiklejohn approached education with different philosophies, yet the beliefs of both reinforced the other so as to provide a rich legacy upon which others could build. Meiklejohn's contributions centered on the structural reform of course programs and their sequencing, as well as curricular reforms related to citizenship and democracy. He created the Experimental Program at the University of Wisconsin, in place from 1927 to 1932, which required students to take a set sequence of courses over two years in order to help them integrate their learning with their real world experiences.

Dewey's contributions are described as teaching and learning innovations, focusing on active learning approaches that were, in current lingo, student-centered and experientially-based. He stressed the dynamic nature of student development rather than seeing students as static vessels into which information was poured. "The particular job of the educational community, as Dewey saw it, was to overcome ever-competitive individualism with interactive cooperation, and this presupposed participation" (Halliburton, 1997, p. 27). Dewey viewed learning as a social process, and as such it is easy to see how learning communities, with their attention to nurturing social and academic development, have a connection with his work (Gabelnick et al., 1990). Issues of competition and individualism still present impediments to learning and can be addressed, in part, through learning communities, especially those that emphasize collaborative activities. Taken together, the curricular and structural reforms of Meiklejohn and the teaching and learning innovations of Dewey provide a solid basis for learning community growth.

In the 1960s, Tussman created a program similar to Meiklejohn's. The "Experiment at Berkeley" was a two-year program of study in which a cohort of students took a predetermined set of courses that were team-taught by a group of faculty (Tussman, 1969). This type of program addressed the weaknesses, as Tussman saw them, of offering courses as discrete units, having little relation to one another. Of individual courses, he wrote:

> The course forces teaching into small, relatively self-contained units. Horizontally, courses are generally unrelated and competitive. . . . They are normally in different subjects, given by different professors, and, with rare exceptions, there is no attempt at horizontal integration. Thus, each professor knows that he has a valid claim to only a small fraction of a student's time and attention. The effect is that no teacher is in a position to be responsible for, or effectively concerned with, the student's total educational situation. The student presents himself to the teacher in fragments, and not even the advising system can put him together again. (Tussman, 1969, p. 6)

Although it lasted only four years, the Experiment at Berkeley is still hailed as an early pioneer of learning community programs, and the report still provides insights for current programs. Tussman's writing captures the revolutionary potential of the learning community movement.

Current literature on learning communities is intertwined with information about collaborative learning strategies, and indeed, the learning community structure provides an ideal environment in which to implement a wide array of collaborative learning strategies. Generally, characteristics of collaborative learning include (a) pairs or

Although collaborative learning can take place in the more traditional classroom setting, the interdisciplinary nature of coursework and the extended contact among students in a learning community intensify the collaboration experience.

groups of students working together to find meaning in, or application of, a course topic; and (b) faculty who are more involved with designing learning activities that promote two- and three-way communication (from student to student, from student to faculty, and from faculty to student) than transmitting knowledge in a one-way avenue of communication (from faculty to student). Although collaborative learning can take place in the more traditional classroom setting, the interdisciplinary nature of coursework and the extended contact among students in a learning community intensify the collaboration experience. (For more information about collaborative learning, see Bruffee, 1993; Goodsell, Maher, & Tinto, 1992; and Kadel & Keehner, 1994.)

Learning communities also have been influenced by two relatively recent paradigmatic shifts in higher education: the shift from a focus on teaching to a focus on learning, and the shift from viewing knowledge as an acquisition of information to the social construction of knowledge. Neither has been rapid, but both place students in more central roles than have previous paradigms. The shift from teaching to learning involves moving away from a preoccupation with what the professor has to say and toward a concern with what students are doing. This change encourages many ways of exchanging information, so that professors are being described as coaches and guides as well as experts at center stage (Barr & Tagg, 1995).

The paradigmatic shift toward the social construction of knowledge has been attributed to a number of sources including the development of feminist studies, constructivist pedagogy, and liberation theory. Its connection to learning communities is evident from the following description:

> Social constructionism, an expanding web of epistemological perspectives in several disciplines, springs from the assumption that knowledge is *socially*—rather than individually—*constructed* by *communities* of individuals. Knowledge is shaped, over time, by successive conversations, and by ever-changing social and political environments. The knowledge business should not be just the territory of competing scholars or experts, the social

> constructionists argue; the shaping and testing of ideas is something in which anyone can participate. (MacGregor, 1992, p. 38)

These shifts in educational philosophy coincide with and support the development of learning communities. Learning communities are vehicles through which professors can make changes in the pedagogy and the structure of courses, and these communities create an environment that encourages faculty development and growth.

Finally, the growth of learning communities has been fueled by the changing financial picture of American higher education. Since the mid-1980s, retention has been the buzzword of administrators faced with shrinking budgets. Any program that can demonstrate an ability to keep students at an institution is looked upon with favor, and so learning communities have gotten their share of attention as effective ways of increasing student retention. The need for better retention has provided an impetus for colleges and universities to consider new programs, and the research generated about the effects of learning communities may be enough to help them gain a foothold into institutional budgets, and eventually into institutional cultures.

How Learning Communities Promote Support for First-Year Students

"Learning communities are attractive because they address, in a myriad of ways, issues of curricular coherence, civic leadership, student retention, active learning, educational reform, and faculty development" (Gabelnick et al., 1990, p. 10). Indeed, learning communities impact many components of student learning and organizational development. Their strengths are the very factors that make it hard to describe them—chiefly, their flexibility and adaptability. Learning communities are non-discipline specific, can incorporate any number of departments across a campus, can make use of existing courses and faculty, and can target any population of students, depending on the courses selected and the services offered/incorporated. They can begin as a top-down administrative initiative, or as a grassroots effort started by small groups of devoted faculty with the help of student affairs professionals.

The effectiveness of learning communities for first-year students is enhanced by the variety of programs that can be incorporated into the learning community format. To address issues of transition to college, learning communities may include an orientation course or some type of freshman seminar. To help students explore their interests, become acquainted with the college's courses of study, and plan their academic career, learning communities may include an advising component. For example, an academic advisor may be assigned to all the students in a learning community and may meet on a regular basis with the group as a whole. Learning communities that include an upperclass student as a peer mentor or peer advisor are designed to assist new students with the social as well as academic adjustments necessary to succeed in college. In each case suggested above, the learning community incorporates the elements of social, emotional, and cognitive development that are important for first-year students. The opportunity to shape the nature of students' first-semester or first-year classroom experiences in a coherent, structured, and consistent fashion can have a wide-ranging influence on their subsequent experiences in college.

Most important to the effectiveness of learning communities, therefore, is their ability to capitalize on the development of the student peer group. Peer group influences in the classroom can have an enormous impact on students' willingness to attend class prepared to participate, to make a commitment to course requirements, and to put aside the anti-intellectual pose that dominates much of student life. Because the peer group influences how students will spend time outside of class, the learning community may be instrumental in determining whether students will be engaged in learning activities versus whether they will pass the time with activities that have little to do with their education. Through collaboration and team teaching, learning communities allow and enable faculty to shape a greater proportion of students' experiences than is possible with individual, unrelated courses. To the extent that they do so, learning communities are an effective way to support the success of first-year students.

Learning communities can be highly effective. Of course, they are not a panacea, nor are they easy to implement. In fact, they are a lot of work! This kind of work involves communication, commitment to others, commitment to course work, and integration of ideas. Learning communities make it possible for students and faculty to pay attention to each other and to learning. Research has shown that increased student involvement in social and academic activities as well as increased student-faculty interaction are two of the most important keys to student success. Learning communities are tools to promote both kinds of involvement, and to the extent that they do, they *will* live up to high expectations.

References

Barr, R. B., & Tagg, J. (1995). From teaching to learning - a new paradigm for undergraduate education. *Change, 27*(6), 12-25.

Bruffee, K. (1993). *Collaborative learning: Higher education, interdependence, and the authority of knowledge.* Baltimore: The Johns Hopkins University Press.

Gabelnick, F., MacGregor, J., Matthews, R. S., & Smith, B. L. (Eds.). (1990). Learning communities: Creating connections among students, faculty, and disciplines. *New Directions for Teaching and Learning, 41.* San Francisco: Jossey-Bass.

Goodsell, A. (1993). *Freshman interest groups: Linking social and academic experiences of first-year students.* Unpublished doctoral dissertation, Syracuse University, Syracuse, NY.

Goodsell, A., Maher, M. R., & Tinto, V. (1992). *Collaborative learning: A sourcebook for higher education.* University Park, PA: National Center on Postsecondary Teaching, Learning, and Assessment.

Halliburton, D. (1997). John Dewey: A voice that still speaks to us. *Change, 29*(1), 24-29.

Kadel, S., & Keehner, J. A. (1994). *Collaborative learning: A sourcebook for higher education, Volume II.* University Park, PA: National Center on Postsecondary Teaching, Learning, and Assessment.

MacGregor, J. (1991, Fall). What differences do learning communities make? *Washington Center News, 6*(1), 4-9. Olympia, WA: Washington Center for Improving the Quality of Undergraduate Education.

MacGregor, J. (1992). Collaborative learning: Reframing the classroom. In Goodsell, A., Mahar, M., & Tinto, V. (Eds.). *Collaborative learning: A sourcebook for higher education.* University Park, PA: National Center on Postsecondary Teaching, Learning, and Assessment.

Perry, W. G. (1968). *Forms of intellectual and ethical development in the college years.* New York: Holt, Rinehart, and Winston.

Tinto, V. (1997). Classrooms as communities: Exploring the educational character of student persistence. *The Journal of Higher Education, 68*(6), 599-623.

Tinto, V., & Goodsell, A. (1993). Freshman interest groups and the first-year experience: Constructing student communities in a large university. *Journal of The Freshman Year Experience, 6*(1), 7-28.

Tinto, V., & Goodsell Love, A. (1995). *A longitudinal study of learning communities at LaGuardia Community College.* University Park, PA: National Center on Postsecondary Teaching, Learning, and Assessment.

Tussman, J. (1969). *Experiment at Berkeley.* New York: Oxford University Press.

University of Miami. (1998). *Transforming campuses into learning communities.* [Conference Brochure] Coral Gables, FL: Author.

Whipple, W. (1987). *Collaborative learning: II.* University Park, PA: National Center on Postsecondary Teaching, Learning, and Assessment.

CHAPTER TWO

Learning Community Models

Anne Goodsell Love and Kenneth A. Tokuno

Learning communities are characterized best by:

> *a. a common cohort of students taking the same classes*
> *b. an interdisciplinary team of faculty teaching courses with a common theme*
> *c. students forming study groups for their courses, spending time socializing outside class, and/or sharing strategies for success*
> *d. collaborative class activities and assignments that require students to work together and intentionally practice skills such as communication, cooperation, and/or conflict resolution*
> *e. all of the above*

In the multiple choice question above, any or all of the answers may best describe a learning community at a particular college or university. Despite seeming so desultory, all learning communities do share some common elements. As mentioned in Chapter 1, the very same strengths that make learning communities possible across a wide spectrum of institutions—their flexibility and adaptability—make them difficult to describe succinctly. This chapter will describe three basic models of learning communities, outline common elements of learning communities, and identify learning communities at specific institutions that address special populations of students.

Learning Community Models

Gabelnick, MacGregor, Matthews, and Smith (1990) described five learning community models that were most prevalent during the late 1980s. Since then, the number of colleges and universities with learning communities has grown dramatically, but the thinking about models has been condensed. MacGregor, Smith, Matthews, and Gabelnick (1997) outline three basic models of learning communities that differ according to the extent to which the student cohort makes up the entire class and the extent to which faculty collaborate. The models vary according to class size, class linkages, and collaboration between students and faculty, but they provide the basic framework upon which many different variations of a learning community can be built. The three models are described below.

Student Cohorts in Larger Classes

In this model, a cohort of students registers for the same sections of two to four courses, but they are not the only students in those courses. Faculty do not coordinate topics or assignments and, indeed, may not change their teaching in any way as compared to their classes without learning community students. Intellectual connections across material and community building may take place in an integrative seminar, where the learning community students are the only students enrolled. Freshman Interest Groups (FIGs) and Federated Learning Communities are some names given to learning communities of this type.

For example, a FIG at the University of Oregon, called International Outlook, groups courses in international relations, world value systems, English composition, and a FIG seminar. Learning community students may be a part of a larger class in the first two courses, and comprise the entire class in the latter two courses. In a FIG, the integrative seminar is led by an upperclass student, and the extent of intellectual connection across classes and community building that takes place is dependent upon the skills of the peer leader and the participation of the students. In a Federated Learning Community, the integrative seminar is led by a "Master Learner," a faculty member who is taking the courses with the students and who models study skills and problem-solving skills for the students.

The model of student cohorts in larger classes enables the student peer group to develop around a common core of courses, but faculty members are not necessarily committed to changing classroom instruction. Often the larger classes operate in the same way whether or not a cohort of learning community students is enrolled. In this way, learning communities can involve courses that, for budgetary or other reasons, cannot be reduced in size. This may help offset institutional resistance to learning communities based on budgetary or other workload concerns.

Paired or Clustered Classes

In this model, courses are paired or linked (sometimes according to a theme); faculty plan the program collaboratively, although they teach their own courses separately. A cohort of students takes the courses together and may be the only students in all the courses. Intellectual connections are made and community building takes place across all courses. For example, courses at Yakima Valley Community College (WA) were linked under the theme of "Biorhythms: Biology, Evolution, and Music as Co-Metaphors" and included biology for non-majors and music appreciation. At Western Washington University, "The Narrative Voice" linked courses in oral history, health, and literature. Paired courses at Temple University do not have a thematic link but are core curriculum courses required of all degree-seeking students.

> Faculty, then, need to be aware of the peer group dynamics and to be ready to take on the role of socializing agent for their students.

Because the learning community students are the only students in all the courses, community building takes on a great deal of significance—there are no other students to buffer the group dynamics that evolve, and no other students to role model appropriate behaviors (this is especially important for first-year students). Faculty, then, need to be aware of the peer group dynamics and to be ready to take on the role of socializing agent for their students. Intellectual connections across courses can be made without the concern that some students are not a part of the cohort. Faculty who have planned a thematic link across the courses can reinforce the topics and expectations of each other's courses; faculty in courses without a thematic link still can reinforce expectations of work quality, student collaboration, and overall classroom behavior.

Team-Taught Program

This model, commonly called a coordinated studies program, is an integrated program of courses that faculty team teach. Students in this learning

10

community model take all their courses together, sometimes meeting as a large group and sometimes meeting in smaller discussion sections or seminars with individual faculty members. All content and assignments are integrated across the theme of the program. Making intellectual connections and building community become inseparable. At Seattle Central Community College (WA), for example, a Coordinated Studies Program called "Speaking for Ourselves: You Cannot Shut Us Out" combined world cultures, non-Western or modern art, English composition, modern world literature, and library research. Living-learning centers often fit this model of team-taught programs as well. Students who live in a common location take courses together which are led by faculty assigned to the living-learning center. Depending on the facilities available, faculty may have offices, courses may be taught, and/or computer clusters or study areas may be set aside within the residence center.

Team-taught programs are the biggest departure of the three learning community models from traditional ways of scheduling and teaching college courses. Structurally, the block of time devoted to in-class work can be arranged and rearranged to fit the goals of the program, not the scheduling plan of the registrar's office. If they wish, the faculty can plan two or more consecutive hours to focus on a particular topic or assignment, invite a panel of guest speakers, or view and discuss a film in one sitting. And team teaching is a radical departure from the norm of a single professor per course. Team teaching allows a variety of perspectives on a topic to be brought forward, providing students with an idea of how an issue can be understood and evaluated from differing points of view. From this, students can learn much more than memorization of facts; they can learn how academic discourse takes place, and how multiplistic views can complement, not just complicate, our understanding of an issue.

These three models—student cohorts in larger classes, paired or clustered classes, and team-teaching designs—can be considered the foundation upon which customized learning communities are built. Depending upon the targeted student population, the amount of departmental and institutional support, and, to some extent, the facilities available, learning communities will take a variety of shapes, even within institutions. Residentially-based learning communities, learning communities for first-year students, and learning communities that incorporate extensive out-of-class activities are examples of the variations possible within these three models.

A useful analogy might be that of making an omelette: The basics needed are eggs, a cooking surface, and heat. Other ingredients may be added to suit the tastes and nutritional needs of whoever is eating the omelette; but regardless of whether it contains meat or cheeses or vegetables, it still can be called an omelette. Similarly, learning communities cluster students in classes, student collaboration is encouraged, and faculty coordinate topics and assignments to varying extents. Beyond that, other "ingredients" may be added to suit the tastes and educational needs of those involved.

Common Dimensions of Successful Learning Communities

Another approach to understanding learning communities is to examine the elements they have in common. Tokuno (1995) describes four dimensions of learning communities: students, faculty, curriculum, and setting. For each, he proposes a continuum along which a learning community could be identified. The dimensions can be independent of one another, but the more developed a learning community is along each dimension, the greater the benefit to the students. Each dimension is described below:

Student Collaboration

To what extent are students clustered so that the learning community facilitates their getting to know one another and promotes interaction for the purpose of learning?

Low level: Students share a classroom, but there is no interaction. If students interact, it is of their own initiative.

| Mid-level: | Might include assigned study groups, a group presentation within a single class, or peer review of writing |

| High level: | All classes are shared; students study together; assignments require collaboration. |

Faculty Collaboration

To what extent do faculty formally interact to discuss issues of learning and teaching, such as specific students they might know, ideas for teaching and evaluation, and curriculum development?

| Low level: | None |

| Mid-level: | Faculty may share information about students and are familiar with what is going on in each others' courses. |

| High level: | Team teaching, daily collaboration on all elements of teaching aside from content, progress and needs of all students are discussed. |

Curricular Coordination

How much are courses, which differ in basic content, integrated so that there is cross- or interdisciplinary bridging? Actual team teaching is not necessary, but increasing levels of integration of curriculum require increasing faculty collaboration.

| Low level: | Courses taught in traditional manner |

| Mid-level: | Two or more classes from different disciplines are linked so that content in one course is related to content in the other course. |

| High level: | Across courses, specific concepts and issues are taught as they are approached by different disciplines. Alternately, subjects are |

taught from a problem-oriented approach, with no discipline identified.

Shared Setting

To what extent are space and other facilities/resources shared by students or other members of the community?

| Low level: | Not at all |

| Mid-level: | Some space is set aside or designated as a place for students to interact (a lounge or library area, for example). |

| High level: | Residential-based learning communities; students live together and take courses based around some learning theme. Faculty may have offices in the residence hall, and/or classes may be held in the residence hall. |

A fifth dimension, interactive pedagogy, can be added to the four dimensions already addressed. It could be argued that this dimension is sufficiently separate from issues of curriculum and levels of faculty collaboration to merit consideration on its own.

Interactive Pedagogy

How is content "delivered" or shared? To what extent are students required to take an active role in contributing to the knowledge base? How much do the faculty encourage or require students to contribute to the learning-teaching process?

| Low level: | Material is delivered primarily in a lecture format. |

| Mid-level: | Collaborative learning strategies such as peer teaching, peer review of writing, or discussion groups are used. Students are expected to contribute to materials presented by the professor to a moderate extent. |

High level: Collaborative learning strategies such as problem-centered learning, experiential learning, and metacognitive activities are used. Students are expected to take an active role in contributing to and shaping the knowledge base to the extent that they research topics for classes, lead discussions, etc.

These dimensions describe learning communities, provide a system for their implementation, and expand the realm of possible configurations, so that a program appropriate to each institutional situation can be created. Educators can examine the placement of a program along any one of these dimensions to see how they might move the program further in the direction of community.

In sum, there is no one "pure" learning community model, nor is there a "best" type of learning community. Judgments as to learning community effectiveness must be made in light of the goals of the program, the student population targeted, and the institutional constraints involved. Many program evaluations have taken place at individual institutions; as the configurations of the learning community models vary, so do the benefits to students, faculty, and institutions.

A Continuum of Collaboration and Integration

A more complex way to understand learning communities is to combine the above dimensions according to the degree of interaction between any two of them. An example is the degree to which they incorporate *integration across courses* and the *complexity of collaboration* involved. Integration across courses reflects the dimension of curricular coordination as described above, and complexity of collaboration could involve either of two dimensions: the extent to which faculty collaborate or to which students collaborate.

Viewed in this way, it is possible to plot various types of learning communities on a grid with a dimension on each axis (see Figure 1). For FIGs, which are examples of student cohorts in large classes, typically have a low level of integration of content across courses, but a moderate amount of student-initiated collaboration (study groups, informal social activities). Thematically linked pairs or clusters may have a moderate amount of integration across courses, and a moderate amount of collaboration, both student-initiated and faculty-initiated. Team-taught programs, such as Coordinated Studies Programs, are designed with the most integration across courses and the most layers of collaboration throughout them, including student- and faculty-initiated activities.

Of course, a limitation of this classification scheme is that it is only two-dimensional, and, therefore, any combination of only two dimensions fails to fully represent the richness and complexity of learning communities. It is difficult to articulate a multidimensional model which might include all of the dimensions of learning communities. The grid used here, however, does allow for a combination of two important dimensions in a model which might best predict student learning outcomes. Of ten possible combinations of dimensions, it is interesting to speculate about which combination would best predict student success.

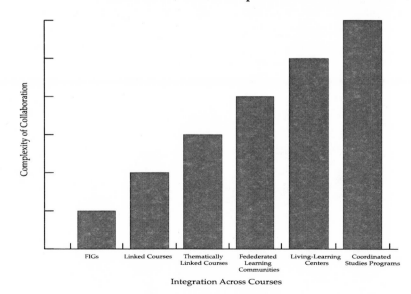

Figure 1. A Continuum of Collaboration and Integration

13

In this model, our prediction is that programs which maximize the dimensions of integration across courses plus collaboration among students and faculty would result in the greatest achievement of learning outcomes.

Learning Communities for Special Populations

To return to the metaphor of a learning community as an omelette, once the basic ingredients are in place (one of the three basic models), other "ingredients" can be added according to the tastes and "nutritional" needs of the students. Learning communities are in place across the country, with many programs designed to address certain subpopulations of students. These special populations of students have needs that are very effectively addressed by learning communities. The various forms of collaboration within learning communities are ideally suited to providing the additional social support and skill development important to the success of such students. This section highlights just a few of the programs that are in place for special populations of students.

Academically Underprepared Students

Some learning communities are composed predominantly or entirely of developmental-level courses, meeting the needs of students who have been admitted to a college or university but have not placed into college-level courses. See the two examples below:

LaGuardia Community College (NY) offers the New Student House, which consists of courses in writing, reading, and oral communication. The program has been in place since 1992 and has a demonstrated track-record of success—students complete and pass their basic skills courses at rates above the average of, and are retained at higher rates than, their non-New Student House peers. There also is an English as a Second Language New Student House for students who need English as a Second Language instruction as well as developmental course work.

Contacts for faculty and curricular development issues are:
Will Koolsbergen

Professor of Humanities and Coordinator of Learning Communities
(718) 482-5496

Phyllis Van Slyke, Professor of English and Coordinator of Learning Communities
(718) 482-5660

Contact for administrative issues:
Harriet Mesulam
Liberal Arts Coordinator
(718) 482-5414

Leeward Community College (HI) offers the PASS Program for underprepared students. This program requires students to commit to spending 30 hours a week together in class or study groups. The same four faculty teach all 80 students, who share four classes (math, reading, writing, and self-development) in "families" of 20 students each. Students also have a set of classrooms and a common study area clustered around the faculty offices.

Contact:
Jack Pond
Professor of Language Arts
(808) 455-0225

Students from Under-Represented Groups

These learning communities may pay special attention to the types of social adjustments needed to be successful in college, as well as providing any type of academic assistance needed. Faculty and staff who can serve as role models are often asked to participate in these learning communities. See the two examples below:

Delta College (MI) offers a program for first-year male students of color called "Which Way is Up?" that addresses the theme of men of color in American culture. The program includes introductory courses in English composition, psychology, and sociology, and a weekly community forum. The forum features a community leader who is invited to talk with the class about the practical application of the psychological and sociological theories being studied. The students, faculty, and community leader have lunch together, which becomes a highlight of the program, and models for students the importance of networking within their community. The program held on Thursday evenings, Friday mornings, and Saturdays is taught by two full-time administrators and one full-time faculty member.

Contact for curricular issues:
Betty Jones
Vice President of Instruction and Learning Services
(517) 686-9299

Contact for administrative issues:
Julia Fogarty
Learning Communities Coordinator
(517) 686-9017

Students with Disabilities

Under the Americans with Disabilities Act, colleges are required to provide equal opportunities to students with disabilities. A number of institutions have special centers or programs designed to meet students' special educational needs. Many of these programs involve student collaboration and exploit some of the better qualities of learning communities. To the extent that: (a) faculty and staff may work together to assist such students, (b) courses may be structured to provide access to learning, and (c) space may be set aside, such programs are true learning communities.

The Komo Mai program at *Leeward Community College (HI)* provides a physical setting for students with disabilities to meet, relax, study, or make use of adaptive equipment. Although there is a self-development course associated with the program, the true value of the program is in creating an environment for the students to feel as if they have a home at the campus, where they have access to all the resources they need.

Contact:
Marie Ruane
Assistant Professor and Counselor
(808) 455-0288

Honors Programs

Many Honors programs function as learning communities, with special sections of courses for honors students, seminars designed for an honors program, or living-learning programs. The College Park Scholars Program at the *University of Maryland* is a thematic, residentially based program for first- and second-year students. Students take a common colloquium, and also take common courses around varying themes such as art, life sciences, or international studies. Most students live in specially assigned residence halls. Each program has a faculty director.

Contact:
Katherine McAdams
Acting Executive Director

Mike Colson
Assistant Director
(301) 314-2777

Residential Students

Living-learning centers take the learning community concept into the residence halls, blurring the lines between in- and out-of-class learning. Classes may be held in the residence hall, and faculty may have offices or even live in the hall. See the two examples below:

The First-Year Program at *St. Lawrence University (NY)* involves students in a year-long, multidisciplinary, team-taught course. Groups of 45 students take the course in common and also live in a common residence area. The three faculty members in the team share advising responsibility for the students and also meet frequently with the residence hall staff to design and support co-curricular programming. Since students share one integrated course as well as live together, it is hoped that they come to realize and appreciate the connections between the many dimensions—intellectual, social, political, and cultural—of their lives.

Contact:
Valerie Lehr
Associate Dean of the First-Year Program
315) 229-5909

Virginia B. Schwartz
Assistant Director of the First-Year Program
(315) 229-5909

Learning Communities at the *University of Missouri at Columbia* are residentially based and incorporate a variety of models. Residence hall floors are organized around academic themes, and everyone in that living unit has expressed some interest in the topic. A freshman interest group (FIG), a subset of new students who take common courses related to the theme, is embedded in each living unit. In addition, students in the living unit may be upperclass students majoring in a related field or students who have participated in that FIG in a previous semester. For example, the learning community called International House includes students in a FIG called "The Global Student." Participants in this program are new students with an interest in international studies, international exchange students, U.S. students who have studied abroad, and students majoring in international studies. Clustering students in this way allows many layers of connections to be made between students, in and around formal curricular structures.

A unique feature of learning communities at the University of Missouri at Columbia is the extent of cooperation between academic and student services units. A core committee shares the responsibility for decision making, issues of implementation, and keeping the large conceptual picture of the program in focus; its members are the Student Learning Coordinator, a Program Coordinator, the Director of Residence Life, and the Associate Dean for Arts and Sciences.

Contact:
Lisa C. Eimers
Student Learning Coordinator
(573) 882-4815

Students with Specific Academic Interests

Students with specific academic majors, especially at small or medium-sized colleges and universities, often are thought of as a learning community because they take many courses together that are required of the major. Nursing and engineering majors often see a great deal of each other, as do students in other science majors. Some institutions, however, take matters further by grouping students in residence halls (as mentioned above), or by offering co-curricular programs and activities for these students. For example, the Women in Science and Engineering (WISE) Program at the *University of Michigan* capitalizes on the common courses that students take as dictated by their majors, and extends academic and support services beyond the classroom as well. For example, although first-year women in science and engineering majors are in large introductory courses, they have labs and discussion sections set aside for them. The WISE Residence Program offers on-campus residence hall housing to 100 first-year women and 25 second-year women; the second-year women act as role models and peer mentors for the first-year women. Also offered through the WISE Residence Program are weekly "WISE Night" programs consisting of professional, cultural, educational, and social activities such as workshops about interviewing skills and resume writing. WISE programs also offer panels of women working in the science and engineering fields and women in graduate programs. Special tutoring is also available to the women in the WISE Program.

Contact:
Cinda-Sue Davis
Director, WISE Program
(734) 998-7225

Conclusion

Concluding this chapter with a section about learning communities for special populations is not intended to suggest that there is any one group of students who is better served by learning communities than another. Learning communities can provide profound benefits to *any* student through the use of shared, connected learning experiences among students and faculty. Learning communities also make it possible for colleges and universities to reorganize faculty work and to restructure the curriculum allowing the faculty, as well as students, to cross disciplinary and departmental borders that traditionally divide them.

Many, if not most, learning communities have been aimed at first-year students, perhaps because such communities create supportive environments for entering students. While not denying this fact, descriptions in this chapter of learning community models show that there are no limits to the applications of learning communities to all students—of any kind, at any level, or in any school of higher learning.

References

Gabelnick, F., MacGregor, J., Matthews, R. S., & Smith, B. L. (Eds.). (1990). Learning communities: Creating connections among students, faculty, and disciplines. *New Directions for Teaching and Learning, 41.* San Francisco: Jossey-Bass.

MacGregor, J., Smith, B. L., Matthews, R. S., & Gabelnick, F. (1997, March). *Learning community models.* Presentation at the meeting of the American Association of Higher Education (AAHE), Washington, D.C.

Tokuno, K. (1995). A conceptual framework for learning communities. Posting to the Learning Communities Leader's listserv (LEARN-COM), and subsequent personal correspondence.

CHAPTER THREE

Garnering the Fundamental Resources for Learning Communities

Jeanine L. Elliott and Emily Decker

As a form of curricular restructuring, learning communities have demonstrated their success in supporting student learning, increasing student retention, and revitalizing faculty[1]. A few simple premises are at the root of reforming part or all of the curriculum into learning community formats, but the activity required to put learning communities into place is different from the day-to-day activities of faculty, academic support staff, and student services staff. Because it is not business as usual, a range of resources is necessary. Learning communities are not inherently costly or time-consuming, but they do require a reorganization of standard operating procedures within most colleges and universities.

The benefits of the learning community approach, particularly for students new to higher education, are becoming so visible in the academy that many institutions are experimenting with various formats, often without considering what resources will be necessary to make them successful. Since the typical college or university is not set up to support these new structures and since the interest and excitement in developing learning communities may come from many different places within the institution, learning community organization will necessarily take many forms. The different components and the resources needed to support these components, can be roughly divided into four areas, each discussed in more detail below:

- The people—the faculty, administrators, academic support staff, and student affairs professionals who are committed to the idea and are doing the work

- The organizational structure—the administrative placement within an institution

- Financial support—the substantive and symbolic uses of money

- The text and context—the purpose of the learning community, the issues the learning community is addressing, and the content of the program

The People

The Building Blocks of Learning Communities

While the knowledge that faculty and staff bring to learning communities is important, other human qualities and their related educational values are equally relevant. Those who are involved in learning community work espouse a commitment to students as they approach their planning and their pedagogy. Effective learning community work requires a strong sense of communalism, collaboration, and connected knowing—a marked contrast to the values of individualism, autonomy, and argument typically espoused by the academy. As the academy is called upon to respond to a wide range of economic, social, and political concerns, it often becomes ambivalent about defining its primary constituents. Faculty, staff, and administrators must work to bridge this values gap if learning communities are to achieve their goals.

Two groups of people are responsible for the initiation and implementation of learning communities. The first resource group is the handful of people who dream, plan, design, and implement learning communities. These educators possess an ongoing commitment to creating collaborative learning opportunities within the academy. They are responsible for selling the dream to others. The second resource group is the larger number of faculty, staff, and administrators who are committed to the idea and who will link the core group with the larger academy through careful, generous translation. People in this second group do many things and have many responsibilities, but the success of learning communities will be dependent on:

- Who is in this group

- Where they are placed within the institution

- Their understanding of the value of learning communities for students, faculty, and institution

- The quality of their relationships with the core planners and teachers

- Their commitment to educational change

Faculty Interest and Commitment

In some institutions, the idea for a learning community starts with a group of faculty who begin collaborating with each other across the boundaries of departments and scheduling blocks. They collaborate because they value this mode of learning for themselves and their students. They have seen the limitations of the current curricular organization, and they envision a learning community design as a way to correct or enrich that curriculum. In such cases, the learning community project starts small and grows in stages. The learning community will thrive and expand if faculty members are able to involve administrators (department and division chairs, academic deans, etc.) and staff (registrar, dean of student services, advisors, etc.) early in the development process.

In the initial stages, the faculty-initiated learning community is partially maintained by voluntary contributions of both faculty and staff and is most likely to come about in institutions that have a culture that supports faculty/staff initiative and creative problem solving. For a time, the satisfaction created by team teaching and collaboration more than compensates for the increased time and energy required by the new methods. Eventually, however, everyone wants to be recognized in some way for work well done; if programs are to remain vital, they cannot be dependent only on the good will of faculty. Intense collaboration creates much of its own energy, but growing programs need increasing administrative and financial support.

To provide for the continued growth of faculty-initiated learning communities, institutions must support the allocation of the following resources:

- Academic administrators, academic support staff, department or division chairs, and

> Intense collaboration creates much of its own energy, but growing programs need increasing administrative and financial support.

faculty curriculum committees who express interest, give support, and are willing to make low-cost, creative changes

- Some staff time designated to assess learning and retention within the learning community

- Support in the development of lines of communication that will include students, their families, and their peer networks so that all will come to understand the purpose and value of learning communities

- Release time or summer grants for faculty/staff planning

- Teaching faculty/staff willing to volunteer necessary time to work collaboratively throughout the teaching period

Practitioners interested in examining faculty-driven learning communities in the community college setting can refer to the *Washington Center News*. The *News* provides a list of community colleges in Washington state where learning communities were initiated by faculty with some administrative support. At four-year institutions, faculty and administrators have developed academic units that offer an alternate curricular structure. Examples include: the law and diversity program at Fairhaven College at Western Washington University, New Century College at George Mason University, and Hutchins School of Liberal Studies at Sonoma State University.

Administratively Initiated Programs

While faculty are a potent force in the formation of learning communities, the initiative for collaborative learning can also begin with the administration. When external funding is involved, the project design may be fully developed before all of the necessary collaborating groups are in place. Unlike faculty-initiated programs, this learning community endeavor may be seen as a discrete project with a beginning and end time. Fundamental questions that arise more organically in a small, faculty-initiated project

will need to be addressed early in the planning process. Some of the first questions that need to be addressed are:

- How will learning communities relate to the mission of this college or university?

- What student, faculty, or institutional problem or issue will the learning community address?

- Which faculty, administrators, and staff care about this problem or issue?

- What core group of faculty can be counted on for an ongoing commitment to the project?

- If that group is not obvious, how can a group be identified and supported as they gain knowledge of and experience with the educational philosophy that supports learning community work?

- How will a secondary support group be developed?

- Who will do the work?

- How will they be rewarded for their work?

Given that the primary resources for learning communities are people, then careful attention needs to be paid to *whom* the teachers will be and how they will *learn* to do this kind of teaching. Some programs do start with the hope that faculty will naturally move from the "I" of the enclosed single classroom to the "we" of interdisciplinary, team-taught, collaborative learning, but it is not necessarily a natural progression. Learning community work requires a shift in focus from sequential learning to contextual learning, from a sequenced series of teachers to a multiplicity of teaching resources, from teaching by experts to teaching through coaching, and from the focus of "what the teacher knows" to "how the student will learn." Finally, an awareness that both faculty *and* students bring knowledge and intention to learning must be fostered. Learning community work requires the full presence of faculty, academic support staff, and learners in the learning event and process.

When a learning community is created by administrative mandate, faculty selected to teach will generally expect to be given extra compensation or release time. Staff may resist the extra work that operating two systems of scheduling, advising, registering, and preparing transcripts requires. If the culture of the institution is non-voluntary, a change in work activities that brings more work will have to be rewarded. There is no way out of it!

Whether the initiative comes from the administration or from faculty, the resources required for learning communities are essentially the same. The difference lies in the timing of when resources will be needed. Administratively-initiated programs will typically require more funding up front while programs based on small departmental initiatives are likely to need funding for growth and expansion. Since resources become part of the motivation for faculty and staff to get involved, they will need to be clearly visible at the outset. They include:

- Clear articulation by key administrators of the value of learning communities and their relation to the mission of the institution

- Professional opportunities for faculty to support necessary changes in teaching modes and styles

- Funding by release time or compensation for faculty/staff planning and teaching

- Adjustment of work responsibilities for academic support staff who have responsibilities related to learning communities

- Changes in administrative structures to facilitate learning community staffing and scheduling across departmental and divisional lines

- An administrative plan for working out full time equivalent (FTE) and student/faculty ratios for learning communities

- Institutional support for an educational program about learning community work for faculty, staff, and students who are unfamiliar with the learning community concept

- Designation of staff time to assess learning and retention in learning community offerings and to evaluate the contributions that learning community work makes to the larger institution

Eventually, attention will need to be directed toward departmental and divisional hiring. Faculty who bring strong interests in interdisciplinary work and in pedagogy will need to be hired. Job descriptions will need to be rewritten and interview questions will need to be crafted to reflect the educational values implicit in learning communities.

Organizational Structure

Cutting across Structural Boundaries

The types of organizational structures for learning communities are as numerous as the institutions in which they exist. Learning communities sometimes start and remain within an already structured unit, such as a particular major, or honors program, or they may become a separate academic unit with their own space and faculty. In either case, learning communities that represent relatively self-contained units reside rather peacefully within the institution. However, most learning communities are organized to work across academic boundaries, some more permeable than others. When learning communities cross boundaries, they have the greatest potential for contributing to educational reform within the institution.

Wherever learning community organizations find their homes, they will need resources designed to facilitate movement and increase collaboration across departmental and divisional boundaries. Some of these resources include:

- One person to serve as a learning community coordinator or a unit director; a present or former faculty member who has taught in learning communities, who can be an advocate in a wide range of campus divisions and areas, and who can determine the impact of any new initiatives on the learning community

- An administrator who thinks both practically and globally about learning communities, and who, with the faculty coordinator, will always remember learning community needs within the context of other campus discussions

- A committee that cuts across the various internal boundaries of the institution and that is representative of the many groups, including students, that have an investment in learning communities

Role of the Learning Community Coordinator

Ideally, the coordinator will have experience teaching in learning communities. He or she needs to have a deep understanding of the educational philosophy embodied in learning communities and their place in the curriculum. The coordinator needs to know the campus thoroughly, to be visible on the campus, and to be seen as a valued member of the academic program. In addition, the person should have excellent facilitative skills to assist faculty work collaboratively on program planning and implementation.

The learning community coordinator must also be a savvy negotiator, skilled in obtaining the personnel and financial resources needed to support the learning community. Solid skills in managing logistical details are also essential. These details include issues of registration, student recruitment, book orders and room scheduling. Questions of compensation, title, and office space should be clearly addressed. Given the complexities and boundary-crossing nature of the coordinator's work, the decision about an appropriate reporting line can be highly

In their very administration, learning communities invite members of the wider campus community to practice collaborative learning!

charged politically. Whenever possible, the learning community coordinator should report to an academic administrator who is also an advocate for learning communities.

Choosing the Academic Administrator

Academic administrators who have primary responsibility for learning communities are often chosen because they value and support these kinds of learning formats, rather than because of their strategic placement within the college and university. If that person is a provost, vice provost, or dean, then his or her authority is usually recognized, even by faculty and staff who do not understand or value learning communities. However, associate deans and division heads have proven themselves as successful advocates for learning community work. In community colleges in the state of Washington, some of these administrators have subsequently become academic vice presidents and even presidents, where their methods of support necessarily change but do not diminish.

Composition and Role of the Coordinating Committee

Dilemmas abound over the structure of a learning community committee. For example, assume that the initial planners want to be sure there is faculty ownership of the program. Each of seven liberal arts departments is asked to select a faculty member to be part of the committee. Five departments select advocates; two send people who are highly skeptical of this new curricular design. In addition to those faculty members, the registrar, the person who schedules classrooms, a classified staff person who hears countless student problems about class selection, the Learning Center director, a librarian, a student recommended by the English Department chair, a dean of student services, and the assistant dean for liberal arts are also named to the committee by the academic vice president. The academic vice president has been the primary advocate for learning communities. Three of the faculty members are relatively

23

new to the campus and have not yet worked on a committee that includes non-faculty. Is this committee too unwieldy? If it is made smaller, key units of the campus will not be involved. Should only advocates be on the committee? Then how will others begin to feel invested? And how will the committee avoid being seen as a self-perpetuating in-group of like-minded people? In other words, there are no simple answers. In their very administration, learning communities invite members of the wider campus community to practice collaborative learning!

Clearly, a learning community committee needs to be organized differently from the usual academic committee; it needs to reflect the values of learning communities themselves. If the learning community is to incorporate multi-disciplinary, collaborative learning, then the committee should incorporate multi-disciplinary, collaborative decision making. Will they know how to do this? It is not likely. A new program may wish to invite a skilled learning community coordinator from another institution to meet with the committee in the early stages regarding collaborative planning and decision making. A committee might also invite faculty who are teaching in learning communities to meet with them periodically; they could discuss together the teaching/learning issues that arise in the classroom as a way of learning more about how to function as a collaborative community. For colleges and universities committed to becoming learning organizations, the organization and work of this committee becomes a prototype for other groups attempting to work across traditional campus structures.

Funding

Cost of Learning Communities versus Traditional Instruction

Different kinds of academic programs require different amounts of money for personnel, space, materials, equipment, student support, and faculty/staff professional development. Learning communities are no exception. However, because most cost differentials are seen as differences between disciplinary programs, justifications for the differentials are accepted. For example, high tech and allied health programs cost more in every way than general education courses for first- and second-year students. Typical cost assessments of learning communities often undervalue the quality of learning that takes place within them for both students and faculty. Furthermore, rather than comparing learning communities with other programs which emphasize student success and learning outcomes, administrators typically compare learning communities with large, multi-section introductory disciplinary courses.

Part of the funding task is to change the focus of the conversation about cost. Heightened learning on the part of both students and faculty is not now included in most cost analyses. Retention of students and student progression is somewhat easier to build into a budget formula, but even that is not common. The learning community coordinator will need to become versed in the way the institution allocates resources to various programs and be able to argue for basic support in language that those who work with budgetary information (i.e., FTEs, faculty/student ratios, and cost per square foot) can understand. Learning how to use current conversations about assessment, student learning outcomes, and accountability to benefit learning community programs is essential.

At the same time, the learning community coordinator should be imaginative enough to propose an expansion of the variables that are ordinarily considered in funding formulas. For example, a faculty member whose stand-alone class becomes part of a learning community approaches the material in that class from an interdisciplinary perspective, using a broader range of pedagogical strategies. In subsequent semesters, the faculty member will be able to teach the stand-alone course from an altered perspective, to the benefit of all students enrolled. So, while these students have not been a part of the original learning community, their learning has been shaped by it. How can these outcomes become part of budget considerations? Our experience in the state of Washington is that inter-institutional, collegial relationships among learning community coordinators can be a powerful force leading to generative conversations about cost.

Learning communities, at their best, cut across budgeting lines. Usually, the budgets for the programs themselves are small. The program is usually dependent upon the good will of others to provide staffing, space, equipment, and student support. Negotiating across departmental boundaries is a skill that must be quickly mastered by learning community faculty and administrators. Learning community coordinators may not want to think of themselves as fundraisers; but, in fact, they learn to play the role. Coordinators often have to negotiate with departmental and unit heads for copying and audio-visual equipment as well as for faculty and staff time. In the early stages, these negotiations will often be informal, but as learning community programs become stronger and stabilized, more formal arrangements need to be made.

One example of financing a program across budgetary lines exists at Bellevue Community College. "Of Mice and Matter" is a learning community that combines chemistry, biology, and study skills, crossing departmental and administrative lines. The faculty load of each person teaching in the program is determined according to different departmental formulas. The chemistry instructor would be expected to teach 48 students, the biology instructor 56, and the study skills instructor, 66. The number of students who participate in "Of Mice and Matter" is 48. The respective departments absorb the difference. Also, at Bellevue, if an instructor is part-time, as the study skills instructor usually is, extra compensation for the increased teaching time is provided through funding from the Interdisciplinary Studies Department, the Science Department, and the Human Development Department. Ratios that are fair from the point of view of faculty in the learning community and of their home departments must be worked out.

In addition to budgetary concerns, learning community coordinators also must negotiate for physical space. Faculty and administrators

> The program is usually dependent upon the good will of others to provide staffing, space, equipment, and student support.

involved in learning community work quickly realize how few spaces on a campus are designed to meet the needs of 50 to 75 students and 2 to 3 faculty working in collaborative modes. Establishing a good relationship with the people responsible for room scheduling can be critical to the success of a program. Some community colleges, several in Washington State, have designed or redesigned areas to create flexible spaces that support collaborative learning. For example, faculty at Lower Columbia Community College designed a cluster of rooms that includes two seminar rooms, a faculty office, and a large classroom furnished with portable chairs and tables, along with cupboards and files that are used to store the accumulating materials from the current learning communities. Because documents from learning communities are filed in the same room, faculty teaching in a given quarter have access to handouts and ideas from other learning communities that are underway at the same time. With the help of supportive administrators, faculty at Seattle Central Community College have several large classrooms designated for learning community use. The rooms are equipped with movable dividers, portable tables and chairs, bulletin and marker boards, computers, Internet access, and other audiovisual support.

The actual budget dollars most often are needed for faculty/staff development and program planning. If funds are available for these purposes within the college or university, then the task is to have some of those funds reallocated to support faculty and staff development in learning communities. Many institutions have seen how the collaborative work done by faculty and staff in learning communities carries over into work outside learning communities. Because of the contribution to the entire institution, administrators can justify spending money for learning community workshops and faculty/staff stipends. General workshops, such as collaborative planning and decision making, interactive teaching and learning strategies, community building, and problem-based, integrative, and experiential learning build expertise among faculty and staff, as well as improving overall teaching skills.

Some institutions work out a system of release time rather than actual dollars to compensate for the extra planning time that collaboration requires. For example, Delta College, a two-year college in Michigan, provides a small amount of release time or a small stipend, a token of the institution's interest in having such programs thrive. This judicious use of funds provides a mark of institutional support, even if only symbolic, that contributes to the general support of learning communities on campus.

Text and Context: What the Learning Community is About

Justification of the Learning Community Project

Discussions about allocating resources for learning communities must be consonant with discussion about the institutional mission. Without an explicit connection to the college mission, learning communities may appear to be an expensive experiment. In these conversations, the tension between traditional individualistic thinking—getting all that you can for your program—will co-exist with communal thinking—supporting the needs of the institution as a whole. Collaborative, boundary-crossing work in the support of learning communities is set in the context of the territoriality of the larger institution; faculty and staff necessarily live in both worlds. Recognizing these tensions as necessary and keeping the conversations about resources productive become the responsibility of all. Without this recognition, arguments over limited resources set people up to lose sight of the advantages of learning communities.

The text and context of the learning community are the central issues in determining resources for learning communities. When financial support is limited, resources need to be directed toward supporting

- The purpose and goals of the program(s)

- Its relationship to the mission of the institution and the undergraduate students it serves

- Improving student learning and faculty vitality

In the fray of day-to-day planning and teaching, the world in which learning communities exist may be forgotten. Learning communities are designed to assist students in making sense of themselves and the world in which they live. If these students are new to the college environment, their immediate world is complex and often intimidating; the demands upon them are many. Young or old, their families and cultures of origin may both support them and drain their energy. The college community contributes a different kind of support and demand on energy; the larger world, another. Developing a way for students, faculty, and staff to rehearse and remember the purposes, goals, and desired student learning outcomes will enrich the experience of everyone.

Reflective thinking about the work of learning communities inevitably produces questions and the recognition of metaphorical black holes. While faculty may assume that their integrative intellectual work creates a coherent whole that students will understand, the students themselves may be struggling to make sense of what appear to be random events. Students often perceive that a particular content or process will not be important to them long-term. Understanding what types of knowledge students value and why can inform the development and assessment of learning communities. While faculty and administrators may be reluctant to enter a conversation with students that calls the value of certain knowledge sets into question, they should view it as another opportunity to engage students in collaborative learning. These conversations that help refine the purpose and goals of the overall program also ensure the continued growth and success of the learning community program.

Conclusion

Over the past 30 years, a variety of strategies and programs have been developed to address a wide array of teaching/learning issues. Adult education, writing across the curriculum, women's studies, area studies, ethnic studies, academic support centers are but a few of the programs that have made a place inside the academy. Each of these programs has, at least in its early years, been dependent "on the kindness of others." These pioneer programs have ranged across the curriculum and the departments, picking and choosing pieces that fit, reshaping those that are not quite right, and creating new ways of integrating and recreating knowledge. Each one has made substantial contributions to the work of the academy.

The development of learning communities is a rather recent phenomenon; the work concentrated in Washington State is just a little over a decade old. Excellent examples of learning community work exist in numerous institutions across the country, but the sharing of information nationally and internationally is just beginning. In addition to learning from each other, we can draw upon the work of earlier integrative, cross-departmental, collaborative programs. We, in turn, can become better prepared to share our knowledge and experience with innovative and experimental programs that arise in the future.

Electronic, Print, and Conference Resources on Learning Communities

- The learning community listserv based at Temple University explores curricular learning communities. To subscribe, send an e-mail message to: *listserve@mv.temple.edu*. Leave the subject line blank. In the body of the message, type "subscribe learncom [your name]."

- The Living Learning Community listserv based at University of Vermont explores residential learning community efforts, some of which have curricular learning communities interwoven in residence life initiatives. To subscribe, send an e-mail message to: *listproc@list.uvm.edu*. Leave the subject line blank. In the body of the message, type "Subscribe icrclle [your name]."

- For a partial listing of curricular learning communities, see the *Directory of Learning Communities*, the webpage of the Washington Center at The Evergreen State College: *http://192.211.16.13/katlinks/washcntr/learncom/index.html*

- *Washington Center News*, published twice yearly, focuses on teaching and learning issues that are related to learning community work. Learning communities, in and outside of Washington, are often featured. The *News* is available at no cost upon request. Send an e-mail request to be added to the mailing list to: *washcntr@elwha.evergreen.edu*

- Regional and national conferences about learning communities are becoming more frequent. Contact the Temple University listserv or the Washington Center for current dates and locations.

Additional Learning Community Resources

Bergquist, W. H. (1992). *The four cultures of the academy: Insights and strategies for improving leadership in collegiate organizations*. San Francisco: Jossey-Bass.

Butler, J. E., & Walter, J. C. (1991). Praxis and the prospect of curriculum transformation. In J. E. Butler, & J. C. Walter (Eds.), *Transforming the curriculum: Ethnic studies and women's studies*. Albany: State University of New York.

Ewell, P. (1997). Organizing for leadership: A new imperative. *AAHE Bulletin, 50,* 3.

Gabelnick, F., MacGregor, J., Matthews, R., & Smith, B. L. (1990). Learning communities: Building connections among disciplines, students and faculty. *New Directions in Teaching and Learning, 41.* San Francisco: Jossey Bass.

Goodsell, A., Maher, M., Tinto, V., Smith, B. K., & MacGregor, J. (1992). *Collaborative learning:*

A sourcebook for higher education. University Park, PA: National Center on Postsecondary Teaching, Learning, and Assessment, The Pennsylvania State University.

Hill, P. J. (1985). Communities of learners: Curriculum as the infrastructure of academic communities. In J.W. Hall & B. L. Kevles (Eds.), *In opposition to the core curriculum: Alternative models of undergraduate education.* Westport, CT: Greenwood Press.

Hill, P. J. (1975). The incomplete revolution: A reassessment of recent reforms in higher education. *Cross Currents, 24,* 424-445.

Laughlin, J. S. (1997). WAC revisited: An overlooked model for transformative faculty development. *To Improve the Academy, 16,* 165-178.

Levine, J. H., & Tompkins, D.P. (1996). Making learning communities work. *AAHE Bulletin, 49,* 10.

Schuster, M. R., & Van Dyne, S. R. (1985). Changing the institution. In M. R. Schuster, & S. R. Van Dyne (Eds.), *Women's place in the academy.* Totowa, NJ: Rowman & Allanheld.

Smircich, L. (1983). Studying organizations as cultures. In G. Morgan (Ed.), *Beyond method:* *Strategies for social research.* Beverly Hills: Sage.

Smith, B. L. (1991). Taking structure seriously. *Liberal Education, 77*(2).

Smith, B. L., & Jones, R. (Eds.). (1984). *Against the current: Reform and experimentation in higher education.* Cambridge, MA: Schenkman.

Smith, B. L. with Smith, M. (1993). Revitalizing senior faculty through statewide initiatives. In *Developing senior faculty as teachers.* San Francisco: Jossey-Bass.

Washington Center for Improving the Quality of Undergraduate Education (1986 to present). *Washington Center News.* Olympia, WA: The Evergreen State College.

Notes

[1]This article arises out of the groundbreaking work of Barbara Leigh Smith and Jean MacGregor, the founding directors of the Washington Center for Improving the Quality of Undergraduate Education, and their reforming colleagues across Washington state. Over the past 14 years, they have designed, implemented, and institutionalized learning communities in over 30 colleges and universities.

CHAPTER FOUR

Planning the Production:
Scheduling, Recruiting, and Registering Students in Learning Communities

Michaelann M. Jundt, Kenneth K. Etzkorn, and Jason N. Johnson

Good theater productions begin with an excellent script and an exemplary cast but must be supported by creative and hardworking set designers, stage crews, and box office staff to ensure a successful run. In the same way, many hands are needed to create successful learning communities; attention to detail behind the scenes is what makes the community possible. Inclusion of faculty, administrators, and student affairs staff in the design and support of student learning opportunities, in the scheduling of courses, and in the recruitment and registration process is critical to the success of learning communities.

The Theater: A College or University

The key to any successful production is knowing the audience. Faculty and staff who are working on learning community design must be aware of the specific set of demographics that define the student body of their institution, especially new students. If the academic preparedness of entering students spans a broad range, the learning community can introduce them to the expectations of an academic community and connect them with appropriate services. In institutions where most students enter with a declared major, the learning community can serve as an introduction to that discipline or department. Large numbers of undecided or premajor students may highlight the need for a learning community that allows students to explore major and career opportunities. Neither of these approaches needs to be exclusive; a learning community can fulfill multiple goals.

Of equal importance to determining the audience is making sure that the performance, or delivery of the learning community, fits the theater. Planners must recognize the strengths and limitations of an institution and work within the environment. Institutions with faculty who are committed to working with first-year students can bring that dedication to bear on the learning community. Those with large numbers of research faculty might find that a group of these faculty is interested in becoming involved with new students. The length of the school term, whether quarter or semester, may impact the design of the course components. For example, if the learning community contains

29

an extended orientation course, the semester system will allow topics to be explored in greater depth. A one-credit course on the quarter system, on the other hand, will provide a cursory introduction to the academic community.

The culture of the institution and its values are important parts of the overall environment. If faculty are eager to collaborate, the design of the learning community can support team-teaching. Where service learning is an institutional value, public service projects, internships, and research can be built into the learning community. Because the use of the World Wide Web and other electronic resources are becoming valued parts of the college curriculum, librarians and technologists are important resources for incorporating information literacy into the learning community.

Bringing the Script to Life: Designing the Learning Community

The first step in developing the structure of a learning community is to spend some time exploring the mandate for and the institution's commitment to the learning community initiative. Because the chance for success of any program is enhanced when the goals are consistent with the mission and goals of the institution, learning community planners may make use of a series of questions to help establish goals and objectives.

- Is the learning community designed to help students feel comfortable and make friends?

- Will the community ensure that students gain critical skills in academic inquiry?

- Does a campus hope to build a community that will sustain itself informally for several years? Is the institution trying to improve retention and graduation rates?

- Are there enrollment goals for the learning community itself?

- Is transition to a major an important theme for learning community students?

The preceding questions are designed to explore the philosophical underpinnings of a particular learning community; however, designers of that learning community must consider practical issues as well:

- *Structure.* How a learning community is structured will impact its academic and co-curricular components. Some models, like coordinated studies programs, require a strong commitment from faculty since design of the curriculum and the teaching will be shared. Course clustering, on the other hand, takes advantage of existing curriculum and general education requirements; however, more effort will be expended in designing the integrative seminar.

- *Theme.* Whether putting together a team-taught coordinated studies program or just linking courses that also stand alone, the theme of the learning community is important in defining the community. For new college students, both general themes and themes with a more specific focus are appropriate. Many students are unsure about their majors, and general exploration is their main goal. On the other hand, many students have a well-defined major or career goal, and they think that they must get started on that track immediately. In either case, students are looking for security. They want to study topics that are vaguely familiar, and they want courses that will "count toward something." By enrolling in general education courses or classes that meet prerequisites for particular majors, students can meet these needs.

An opportunity exists, however, to balance students' ache for the familiar with expo sure to new disciplines and unfamiliar ideas. What better way for students to risk exploration of unchartered territory than within the safety of a learning community? Sometimes the theme or title of a learning community may soften the fear of the courses within it. Paired with history and called "The Ancient World," a classics course becomes quite enticing. Coupled with economics in a "Business" learning community, a speech course may not appear so daunting.

- *Student Resources.* Current students can provide valuable insight about course content and the amount of work involved in a particular class—useful information when putting together clusters of courses. These same students will have ideas about faculty who might work well within a learning community as well as opinions on which classes should be linked together. Ideally, it is a good idea to include undergraduates in learning community planning whenever possible. They can move from being participants as freshmen to assisting in the development and leadership of communities as upper-division students.

Each Freshman Interest Group (FIG) at the University of Washington includes a one-credit course entitled "University Resources, Information, and Technology" taught by an undergraduate peer instructor. These peer instructors go through a competitive selection process and rigorous training program. As students who have successfully navigated their way through the institution, developed their own communities, and balanced school with various co-curricular and extracurricular activities, upper-division peer instructors have excellent ideas about what new students need upon entering college. Faculty and administrators should tap into their enthusiasm and unique knowledge base.

> Learning communities can . . . give undecided students the opportunity to explore fields that are new to them, both through their classes and out-of-class activities.

Music and Costumes: Adding Value to a Learning Community

Music and lighting can make the difference between a mediocre performance and a spectacular one. These production values often set the tone for the show and work to engage the audience. In much the same way, designers of learning com-

munities need to build in different components of community building and learning activities to engage their audience. A variety of academic and co-curricular activities can be built into a learning community, and these activities should reflect the strengths and culture of the institution. For example, if all first-year students live on campus, it may make most sense to locate learning communities within residence halls. Or administrators may choose to center the learning community outside the residence hall so that it becomes a common ground for resident students, those involved in Greek life, and commuters. If students enter the university within a major or department, the departmental community may be part of their learning community experience. At institutions where most majors are competitive and students must work toward completing prerequisites, a learning community could emphasize academic planning. Learning communities can also give undecided students the opportunity to explore fields that are new to them, both through their classes and out-of-class activities. Where service learning or undergraduate research is a part of the culture, the learning community experience can introduce students to this part of the institution's mission.

Many times, the way these components are incorporated into the learning community has the biggest impact on students. Through a structured but flexible curriculum, students can find what they need and begin to build their own communities. Student-generated communities may center on projects, discussion or study groups, or e-mail discussion lists. Whatever form the community takes, it contributes to student learning both about a specific discipline and the university in general. Through meetings with advisors, informal talks with faculty, and interviews with professionals in a given field, students also are introduced to a larger learning community beyond their immediate peer group.

While some aspects of community will develop naturally, others must be engineered. Questions such as "who will be responsible for the design and implementation of the engineering plan?" and "what activities can be used to facilitate the community-building process?" must be answered by the learning community planning group. Discussions of opportunities and events may happen informally with more experienced students, especially in coordinated studies programs. If a learning community is being built around a cluster of courses, a first-year experience course taught by a faculty member and a student or a student affairs professional may be included.

One important aspect of community is that it provides its members with a support system; however, community planners must be explicit about the kind of academic support the learning community will provide. This includes defining the role of the learning community peer leaders. Some students may expect that leaders will serve as tutors, but tutoring 20 students is nearly impossible. Leaders will need to help students reframe their expectations in regard to tutoring while helping them develop strategies for academic success. They can direct students to campus resources such as writing centers, library services, and technology tools. They can discuss time management techniques and study skills.

> Departments that are looking to recruit students value the opportunity to introduce themselves to new students by linking an introductory course from their discipline to a related course in a more familiar subject.

and necessary support systems. Many campuses have centralized advising for new students, but advisors and curriculum planners from particular departments should also be involved in learning community planning. (The roles of academic advisors in learning communities are explored in Chapter 8.)

In working with academic departments that already serve significant numbers of freshmen, planners should explore what the learning community can offer them. A learning community gives faculty the opportunity to adjust their courses so that they dovetail with other courses. Maybe the history department has always wanted to try having students co-enrolled in art history or classics courses. A campus-wide learning community coordinator helps departments investigate ways to link courses, thereby exposing students to information they would not have gotten otherwise. Putting together a package of courses can help departments in other ways. Science departments are eager to include their difficult-to-schedule lab times in prepackaged clusters. Departments that are looking to recruit students value the opportunity to introduce themselves to new students by linking an introductory course from their discipline to a related course in a more familiar subject.

The Stage Crew: Working with Others to Build Learning Communities

While it is best for one or two people to have the oversight for scheduling the learning community courses, asking for input from around campus builds support for the program and usually makes for a more comprehensive approach. Good directors consult with producers, performers, designers, and musicians before announcing "Action!"

Academic advisors, especially those who work most closely with first-year students, must be key players. They can advise planners about student goals and interests, the most sought after classes,

The structure of the institution and the kind of learning community being created will determine how much faculty involvement is needed. In some cases, faculty just need to agree to have their course clustered with other courses without changing how they teach the course. At the other end of the spectrum, faculty may be making a commitment to team-teach in a learning community, which involves many hours of planning and collaboration.

At the University of Washington, the FIG program has been running so long that some assumptions are made. For example, FIGs always include sections of sociology, psychology, history, political science, chemistry, math, and English, no matter who is teaching them. Sometimes instructors are not assigned to teach fall quarter courses until late in the summer, long after planning must be completed. This highlights an important factor built in to the University of Washington FIG program and others like it: They are course driven, not faculty driven. At an institution that does not have an undergraduate core curriculum, the learning community can appeal to first-year students by incorporating courses that fit within the broad, general education guidelines. Students are looking for introductory courses upon which they can build. At this point in their careers, they are not always as concerned about which faculty are teaching these courses.

Faculty and other instructors, including graduate student teaching assistants, may have some concerns about the way community develops in their classes. Planners need to anticipate these concerns so that they can assist faculty when problems arise. In a successful community, a high level of comfort and shared interest will exist among the participants. An instructor can make use of this closeness in class discussions, peer review, and group processes. This closeness and support may also empower students to protest something they do not like about a class; however, since they are new to the university environment, the students' frustration may be expressed inappropriately. Before the term begins (or very early in the quarter or semester), bringing new and experienced learning community faculty together so that they can share ideas and strategies can help alleviate concerns and point out new and creative teaching strategies.

At the same time, planners should help faculty understand the kinds of instruction and modeling that the peer leader will bring to the group. In fact, spending some time with faculty talking about the role of the peer leader and how that student contributes to the overall goals of the program is time well spent. Directors of first-year learning communities can play an important role in helping to remind the rest of the campus community about the transitions that new students face. Yes, freshmen arrive every September, but their transition experience may last well beyond the winter break.

Not only are traditional college freshmen adjusting to a new, often more rigorous, academic routine; but they are also re-evaluating their own identity, developing new relationships, and being confronted with new ideas and perspectives. Peer leaders can be a stabilizing influence during this chaotic time. Not only can they be there for the students in times of crisis, but the peer leaders can also model effective approaches to the academic environment

A Winning Theater Season: Scheduling Learning Communities

The key to scheduling the courses that will fit into learning communities is developing and maintaining strong relationships with academic departments and the registrar. If new students are registering after continuing students or if they are registering on a staggered basis before the term begins, sections of courses must be reserved for learning communities. Although course structure and scheduling techniques may vary from campus to campus, most institutions will work within one or more of the following scenarios.

Reserving an Entire Course

Most clustered learning communities include a combination of small courses (equaling the size of the community, usually between 20 and 30 students) and larger courses where the learning community students are a subset of all the students enrolled in the course. With small courses, it is just a matter of reserving them for the learning community so that other students—those not committing to the community—cannot sign up. At Temple University, learning community classes are identified with a special section number. This serves as an identifier for students, faculty, and advisors while reserving the section of the course for the learning community students.

Reserving Sections of Courses

Most institutions have some large lecture courses that regularly meet in small discussion sections. If a group of learning community students is going to be a subset of a large course, reserving one of these discussion sections is the easiest way to structure it. This technique gives the discussion group instructor—often a graduate student teaching assistant—the opportunity to build upon the group's cohesion and mutual interests.

Creating Sections of Courses

In some cases, large lecture courses do not have built-in discussion sections. At the University of Washington, creating a "dummy" section of a large lecture course and reserving it for FIG students has worked well. For example, Psychology 101 section A does not break down into discussion sections and it enrolls 500 students. A discussion section, labeled section B, is created and reserved for 20 FIG students. Students enrolled in section B meet jointly with section A—same time, same room, same instructor—but they also meet separately as a discussion group. The enrollment of section A is lowered from 500 to 480 to accommodate FIG participants.

Lowering Course Enrollment Limits

Similarly, lowering the enrollment limit of a course makes it possible to enroll learning community students without reserving an entire section. To do this, an institution must have the flexibility to add students to courses above the stated limit of the course. For example, a UW business FIG might include an entire section of English composition, one of the discussion sections of a large macroeconomics course, and a portion of a math course. If the FIG has 20 students and the limit of the math course is 40, the registrar might lower the math class limit to 20 in the online system while keeping the room assignment the same. This way, 20 continuing students (who register for classes in the spring) could sign up for that math section. Over the summer, as students sign up for this business FIG, they are added to the math course. These 20 FIG students give the course a total enrollment of 40. Clearly, there are many ways to handle scheduling for a learning community. The key is to design a system that works within the parameters of the institution's current registration system.

The Box Office: Recruiting Students to Participate in a Learning Community

Attracting an audience for this production begins with the program itself. Students need to know what a learning community is and what the benefits of participation are. Current and former learning community participants are excellent marketing resources because they have experienced the value of the learning community firsthand.

Identifying the needs and interests of the audience will also make the marketing and recruiting plan more effective. Sometimes the idea of community and the activities that support it are most appealing to students. Questions important to the student include:

- Will I meet other students with similar interests?

- Will I have the guidance of an experienced student?

- Will I learn about campus resources and opportunities, have close contact with a faculty member?

- Will the learning community help me find a niche?

The answers to these questions may be more important to a student than the courses comprising the community.

However, courses are important to students, and most will approach orientation or the first advising assignment eager for an answer to the question, "What classes should I take?" Planners need to determine which classes will draw students toward a learning community. Building in high demand or popular courses can be effective. If it is difficult to get into a calculus course, planners should consider adding it to the learning community. At the University of Washington, it seems that everyone wants to take "Sociology of Deviance." Therefore, when this particular course is in a learning community paired with an ethnic studies class—a course that, for whatever reason, does not attract many first-quarter UW freshmen—students line up to take it. Students also worry about fulfilling requirements; therefore, building the learning community curriculum around the undergraduate core can be an effective way to structure the first year. Student interests, restricted course offerings, and general education requirements should be considered when designing the learning community. The bottom line—if learning communities offer courses of interest to students and help them stay on track for completing a degree, students will be more likely to enroll.

All learning community programs—whether just starting or well-established—need to pay attention to effective recruiting techniques. Much time is spent determining how to talk with new students about learning communities, but many admissions professionals will confirm that many prospective students are quite interested in learning communities. In fact, the presence of learning communities may be one factor that draws students to a campus. When putting together materials about the learning community program, it makes sense to ensure that these publications are accessible to prospective students. First, students must receive information about the program. Mailings to newly enrolled students to pique interest and a registration process that fits with the campus orientation and advising system are critical. Because parents are vitally interested in quality learning experience for their students, they should also be informed about the program. A third group that planners will want to make sure has the entire learning community picture is the advising and orientation staff.

As mentioned before, the title or theme of the learning community is critical. Most students are savvy consumers, and, like most of us, they are drawn to creative presentation. At the same time, because a learning community's audience members—new students—are really making a commitment to become the players, truth in advertising is critical. Students must know what will be

... the title or theme of the learning community is critical. Most students are savvy consumers, and, like most of us, they are drawn to creative presentation.

expected of them. Information about the amount of reading and writing required in an introductory international studies course, for example, will not deter those who are really interested in international relations but will give pause to those students who are drawn only to the packaging.

Ideally, a marquee becomes a fixture on Broadway. Hopefully, learning communities begin to build that same kind of presence on campus. In order for this to happen, a significant number of students must participate regularly in the program. These same students (and others who are interested) must be brought in as upper-division students to be peer leaders or to help the coordinators plan and revise the communities. At the University of Washington, FIGs have been running for over ten years. Almost 2000 students, approximately 45% of the first-year class, were enrolled in FIGs in Fall 1998. In addition to serving a large number of entering students, upper-division students (approximately 90 in Fall 1998) have significant involvement in the program delivery either as peer instructors or as student coordinators in the director's office.

Even as learning communities become built into students' experience at an institution, coordinators should not underestimate the power of word of mouth: Siblings, friends, parents, and roommates all hear about the learning community experience. Students who previously participated in the community as well as undergraduates who served as peer leaders are going to talk about their experience whether it was positive or negative. A quality program builds its own legacy.

Season Ticket Sales: Registering Students into the Learning Community

Good theater companies know that viewing a stage production extends beyond the footlights to the house staff. The theater itself must be warm and inviting. Once potential audience members have been sold on the show, the process of purchasing tickets and finding their way to their seats should be well organized and seamless from their perspective. The same is true for students who are registering for learning communities. While the process of clustering classes or reserving sections may be logistically difficult for the institution, it should appear transparent to the student. The best way to begin institutionalizing a learning community program is to build the registration process into the existing orientation, advising, and registration system. Clearly, involving academic advisors and orientation staff is critical to making the system work.

Depending on how an institution approaches advising and registration, a learning community can ease advising pressures. Since many learning communities include general education courses and major prerequisites, students may not need the approval of an advisor to register for a community. At the University of Washington, advising is not mandatory, but professional academic advisors are available during new student orientation to meet with members of the first-year class who request an advisor. Many UW freshmen who sign up for a FIG do not see an advisor during orientation, thus easing the burden on the advising staff. This paves the way for including academic planning—and specifically, advising—into the learning community. At some institutions, it may be appropriate to have an advisor affiliated with each learning community.

If registering students for a cluster of courses, some kind of "master" schedule number is helpful. One registration number could trigger registration in the three or four courses that make up the community. However, the more labor-intensive, manual system will work too, even for large programs. At the University of Washington, students sign themselves up—via telephone registration—for one course using an entry code obtained from FIG representatives at orientation. Every institution needs to have a way—through entry codes or some other system—of monitoring how many students are in each group. Once students have registered for this one course, indicating their commitment to the group, then the FIG administrators add the students into the two or three other courses in their cluster. It takes time and good attention to detail, but it can be done.

Planners will also need to consider specific populations of students when recruiting and registering and whether any flexibility will exist with the course clusters in certain situations. Students with admissions deficiencies or those at academic risk may require different courses than those in the mainstream. Student athletes, especially those participating in fall sports, may need a lighter credit load. Working with campus support services will help ensure that all students' situations are taken into account.

As the program grows, one unfortunate side effect may be frustrated students and parents who were unable to enroll in the learning community program due to space limitations. Planners will want to consider whether other learning community opportunities will be available for freshmen or whether the program will be repeated in the winter or spring quarters. Developing a priority system and a plan for expansion at the outset may reduce the number of public relations problems that are sometimes associated with high-demand programs.

The Reviews

Opening night reviews often dictate the future success of a new Broadway show, but the initial reaction to a learning community is not an adequate measure of its success. A well-designed, ongoing evaluation process ensures a long and strong life for learning communities by providing information designed to improve the program. Planners should solicit feedback from students enrolled in the program, and they should also talk regularly with faculty, student leaders, and other administrators.

Even if learning communities are a fixture on a campus and almost everyone supports their continued existence, it is important to bring people into the conversation when considering changes to the program. When looking for new disciplines to incorporate into learning communities or when searching for ways to bring together different groups of students, faculty members must be involved in the conversation. The University of Washington FIG program is launching an aggressive expansion plan; and for the first time in the twelve-year history of the program, we are convening a campus-wide advisory committee, composed of faculty, departmental administrators, and academic advisors.

Learning community planners must remain open to suggestions and should cultivate a network of learning community colleagues at other colleges and universities upon whom they can call for advice. Initial plans for the learning community must include goals and objectives as well as measures that will indicate whether these goals are being met. To garner continued support for the learning community project, the entire campus community should be aware of the goals set and the progress being made toward those goals. Statistical data is important— number of students, persistence rate, grade point average—but anecdotal evidence can be just as compelling. The campus community will be pleased to see increases in retention and student academic success, but they will become engaged and excited about learning communities if they hear students' personal stories and how the learning community helped shape those stories. While positive evaluations of the learning community will help resell the campus on the idea, the compiled data, both positive and negative, provide a rich ground upon which improvements can be made.

CHAPTER FIVE

Teaching and Learning in a Learning Community

Diane W. Strommer

In 1969 I accepted my first teaching position at Boston University in the College of Basic Studies (now the College of General Studies). I was to teach rhetoric, a difficult assignment for a new Ph.D. in renaissance drama to accept, and in a structure that did not resemble anything I had previously encountered in my undergraduate or graduate school experience. Nonetheless, for pragmatic reasons I accepted the position, though with less than complete enthusiasm.

I did not realize it at the time, but that teaching experience profoundly shaped my thinking about higher education and student learning, about what teaching could be, about the students we serve, about the value and importance of community—for students and for faculty. BU's College of Basic Studies was structured as a collection of learning communities, mini-colleges we used to call them. Five faculty members, each representing a division of the curriculum—humanities, social sciences, sciences, math, and rhetoric—were assigned to a teaching team of 120 students who were further subdivided into four sections. The faculty team met weekly to discuss our students' progress, to provide coherence in the curriculum, and, in those difficult times of the early 1970s, to figure out ways we could make connections not just among our disciplines but also between the books we taught and the world our students experienced. Our challenge was to understand our students and by understanding them to create relevance, overcome boredom, compensate for uneven preparation, and engage them so that they would substitute their habit of immediate gratification for the long-term rewards of learning.

We felt that the relationships we forged with one another and with our students were well worth the price we paid in hours of long, hard work. It was, as the Peace Corps motto goes, "the toughest job I've ever loved." What I did not realize then, or for a long time afterward, was that the challenges presented by the atypical students in the College of Basic Studies during the early 1970s would increasingly become the norm in American higher education.

As an academic administrator and faculty member at Texas A&M University a few years later, I tried to recreate the benefits of community and coherence on a much smaller scale in a large and growing university. The title of the program, The English/History Project, may have been uninspired, but the results were not. Initially funded by the National Endowment for the Humanities, the program was based on a simple idea: Sections of the required writing course were linked to large sections of the required course in American history. Faculty members met and developed interwoven syllabi, and classes were scheduled concurrently so that two-hour blocks of time could be used on occasion for a guest lecturer, film, or other events. The content of history formed the basis of students' composition assignments as they developed skills in writing, reading, and research. We encouraged their studying together and hoped that other connections would result from being part of a relatively small group together in both a small and a large class.

Neither of these programs was called a *learning community*, but that, of course, is what each was in some sense of the term. As my experience illustrates, in both their simple and more elaborate forms, an old model has become new, and structures that link courses, faculty, and students have been reinvented and reenergized to meet new student needs and new conditions of higher education.

The needs of today's students are different, and in some ways more pronounced, than the students I knew in the early 1970s. We certainly know a great deal more now about how students learn best and the most effective strategies for teaching them than we did 20 or 30 years ago. Other conditions have changed as well, and external forces make it difficult to continue with business as usual despite the conservative tendencies of institutions. Stringent budgets, political and parental concern about the extent to which students are acquiring the skills they need for a changing workplace, and demands for accountability all have fostered a climate for experiment and change. Perhaps most importantly, as Peter Ewell points out, "solid research on how learning really occurs, on how it can best be facilitated, and on how the organizations that foster it should be structured has burgeoned over the last ten years—especially in the revolutionary field of cognitive science" (1997, p.1).

The literature on learning informs our understanding of why learning communities are an effective structure for improving student success. A literature review of cognitive psychology also highlights strategies that can make learning communities more effective. Several summaries of the major insights from cognitive theory, in particular Angelo (1993) and Ewell (1997), are helpful in understanding what researchers have discovered. The following summary of "What Research Says about Improving Undergraduate Education" (1996) draws upon the discipline of cognitive science and offers a litmus test for programs intended to promote learning.

Quality begins with an organizational culture that values:

1. High expectations

2. Respect for diverse talents and learning styles

3. Emphasis on early years of study [i.e., first and second undergraduate years]

A quality curriculum requires:

1. Coherence in learning

2. Synthesizing experiences

3. Ongoing practice of learned skills

4. Integrating education and experience

Quality instruction builds in:

1. Active learning

2. Assessment and prompt feedback

3. Collaboration

4. Adequate time on task

5. Out-of-class contact with faculty

Our increased understanding of how people learn best owes a debt to the important and widely published work done by Gabelnick, MacGregor, Matthews, and Smith (1990) and others at the Washington Center and to the research of Vincent Tinto and his associates (1994, 1993); but this does not fully account for today's interest in learning communities. Rather, campus experiments with learning communities are flourishing because many faculty sense that this structure promises an effective way to address some of the most pressing concerns of the academy—disengaged, passive, and unevenly prepared students, a fragmented curriculum with little connection between and among courses, and a high freshman to sophomore year attrition rate. Faculty teaching general education courses further observe the vocational bent of today's first-year students, who seem "to believe that an education is to be endured rather than enjoyed" (Gose, p. A37).

The annual survey conducted by the Higher Education Research Institute at UCLA, under the direction of Alexander Astin, finds some students reporting that they were frequently bored in high school classes, had little contact with teachers outside of class, spent fewer hours on homework and more hours working, and were uncertain about their skills in math, reading, and writing. These are the same students for whom general education courses are a series of hurdles to be jumped as quickly as possible in their race to a degree and a career. In the majority of our colleges and universities, students are unattached, uninvolved. Fewer live on campus; fewer participate in extra-curricular activities. Class absenteeism has reached epidemic proportions in some institutions, particularly in large lecture classes. And despite multiple retention programs, attrition rates seem hard to improve.

The promise of creating or recreating a community, particularly one centered on learning, that would solve these problems is thus very appealing to many faculty. It is important, however, to be very clear about what exactly it is that we are promulgating, what we mean by a *learning community*. As one person commented on the learn-

ing communities listserv (learncom@vm.temple. edu), "just linking courses doesn't do it." Even the following definition from the pioneering Washington Center is ambiguous about critical details such as classroom practice:

> Learning communities are intentional curricula restructuring efforts that thematically link or cluster classes during a given term and enroll a common cohort of students. Learning communities aim to provide students with greater curricular coherence, and to provide both students and faculty an opportunity for increased intellectual interaction and shared inquiry.

> While interdisciplinary and collaborative learning are often components of learning communities, free-standing courses on interdisciplinary topics, or free-standing courses in which collaborative learning occurs, are not in and of themselves learning communities as we define them. It is the reorganization of students' curricular lives that is key to the creation of intellectual and social community. (*News*, p. 22)

As important as clear definitions and research are to understanding learning communities and their value, however, we also recognize that a lot of what happens on campus and in classrooms is *ad hoc*. By collecting some ideas and experiences from faculty actually engaged in teaching in a learning community, we can more carefully frame our own goals and prepare for the rewards and hazards of teaching in a learning community.

Discovering Faculty Perspectives

I developed a brief questionnaire in order to gather information and impressions from faculty teaching in a learning community. I hoped to find themes that could be woven into a useful framework for others interested in teaching in learning communities on their campus. Aside from basic demographic data, the questions were

The promise of creating or recreating a community, particularly one centered on learning, that would solve these problems is thus very appealing to many faculty.

open-ended. I distributed the questionnaire primarily through the learning communities listserv and to faculty involved in learning communities projects at the University of Rhode Island and Rhode Island College. I received 48 usable responses from about two dozen different institutions, including public and private colleges at all levels. Several institutions shared their internal assessments with me, and I have drawn from their findings as well. Neither the survey I conducted nor the results I summarize can be characterized as a quantifiable research project. My goal was to collect anecdotal responses that would yield practical classroom strategies not to measure systematically the success of those strategies.

Respondents were all faculty currently teaching in a learning community at an institution of higher education—community colleges, small private colleges, large public colleges and major universities. Virtually all were highly experienced, many having had 20 or more years experience in college teaching. They were in the middle of their careers and beyond, most in their 40s and 50s. Such mid-career faculty are most likely to find the experience of teaching in a learning community to be rejuvenating and thus make good recruits to staff new learning community programs. The requirement to achieve tenure through research and publication makes it very difficult for young, new faculty to risk their careers by devoting the time to teaching that is required in a learning community.

How Faculty Define the Learning Community

Just what can be termed a learning community? The three basic types of learning community models include (a) student cohorts in larger classes such as "Freshman Interest Groups" (FIGs), (b) paired or clustered classes (e.g., The English/History Project mentioned earlier), and (c) team-taught programs (MacGregor, Matthews, Smith, & Gabelnick, 1998). As my respondents indicate,

... "a learning community creates an academic and social community of learners who share ideas across disciplines; the community includes both faculty and students who are all engaged in the learning process . . ."

the number of adaptations of these three basic models are many. Although sometimes the answers reflect a lack of clarity about the goals of a learning community ("I don't really know," or "We're still trying to figure this out"), most emphasize developing relationships between faculty and/or students, restructuring the curriculum, or using different teaching/learning methodologies.

We recognize that one of the major tasks for beginning students is finding their place socially as well as academically. Given the increased number of working and commuting students, making friends on campus is harder than it once was; therefore, many learning communities emphasize developing relationships between and among students. As one faculty respondent writes, a *learning community* is "a group of students who experience classes together. They share information, knowledge, emotions, review sessions, successes, and disappointments. In many cases, friendships evolve which may last a lifetime." Another suggests a similar definition of a *learning community* as "a group of learners who spend the greater portion of their academic day together, experiencing the same classes, instructors, assignments, and trials and tribulations of beginning college students."

The research findings of Astin (1993) and Pascarella and Terenzini (1991) stress the significance to student learning of the peer group and of contact with faculty. That important relationship between faculty and students is fostered by many learning communities. Some respondents emphasize the collaborative nature of their learning community as "a group of students and teachers working together," or "a group of students and teachers engaged in the learning process together." Another writes, "a learning community creates an academic and social community of learners who share ideas across disciplines; the community includes both faculty and students who are all engaged in the learning process. For me, writing is always part of the learning community."

Other responses emphasize the way in which learning occurs, the structure of the class. The learning community thus is "a class or group of students who, in smaller groups, are encouraged to work together to enhance the learning process for each individual member." For them, the focus on learning as a cooperative or collaborative activity among peers is primary; a *learning community* is "a group of learners at different levels of discovery who work together to explore the connections between a variety of content areas or disciplines." For still others, a learning community is primarily a structure, "a formal linking of classes taken by a cohort of students, a unique structure that makes for more interaction between students and faculty."

Teaching Strategies

Good teachers generally use a "mixed method" approach to teaching, and respondents to my questionnaire reflect that variety. Relatively few report using "straight lecture" in any of their classes, although about a third rely primarily on lectures punctuated several times during the lecture period with activities. Discussion and small group activities were other frequently used methodologies for both their regular and learning community classes. Although most faculty report that they do not change their basic teaching strategies for the learning community, their comments about the benefits of student participation suggest that many do, in fact, expand their repertoire even if they do not make major changes.

Advantages and Disadvantages of the Learning Community

Advantages of a Learning Community for Students

On many campuses, assessments support the claim that learning communities benefit students, particularly first-year students. In a learning community, students are more likely to feel validated as college students—"they feel being a student is a positive experience"—a feeling particularly critical to the success of first-generation college students (Rendón, 1996). Collaborative learning is more likely, another faculty member observes, when a social community is created that fosters study groups, peer teaching, shared knowledge. Another respondent comments that students seem "more comfortable about speaking up because they aren't isolated as they are in a free-standing class." Several respondents note improved class attendance and reduced attrition, stemming from group support for "everything from academic difficulties to child care. Academic success generally improves in a setting with such support. Students feel more connected, less isolated and alone." Academic skills also improve, and in many communities an "integration of content material and skills across disciplines" develops. In a learning community, "connected learning, less fragmentation of information, integrated skills, critical thinking skills, creative applications, and improved synthesis of information" are emphasized in teaching practice.

Disadvantages of a Learning Community for Students

Although most faculty report that the many social and academic advantages of learning communities to students far outweigh their disadvantages, the latter do exist. The two major problems reported suggest that unusual skill and care (and time) need to be devoted to building and monitoring groups and establishing an appropriate classroom climate. One faculty member worries that the "learning community can reinforce a 'secondary school' mentality in which students band together and maintain an adversarial role in regard to the authority figure, the instructor." Others mention cliques forming in the class, with a number of students bonding closely but leaving out others. Faculty respondents who teach only freshmen note that "they don't always have a sense of college decorum and don't have upper-class students as models" leading to "the adopting of less than desirable habits (skipping class)." Even so, most find that the advantages to students of the small group far outweigh these potential problems

Several faculty noted that students have to work harder and are "forced to take academics more seriously," which they may see as a disadvantage. Others expressed concern about a post-learning community "funk," disappointment when their other college experiences don't offer the same coherence, opportunities for collaboration, or support. Learning communities that link three or four courses also reduce student choice in course selection and may make participation difficult for part-time or working students who have less flexibility in scheduling.

Major Advantages for Faculty

More than one promising innovation in higher education has faltered because it lacked sufficient faculty endorsement to be sustained over time. Based on their experiences, the comments of faculty on why teaching in a learning community is valuable to them center on establishing different relationships with students and colleagues and what they learned because of that difference. Not only do faculty comment on "the opportunity to gain more insight into individual students through shared experiences," but they also report that the learning community provides the opportunity for a "much greater appreciation of the freshman experience," a chance "to keep in touch with *real* student issues." This they find "intrinsically valuable" in creating better connections with all of their students. It improves teaching, as one respondent says, by "grounding it in experiential realities."

Being able to discuss individual students with colleagues fosters understanding. One faculty member reports, "Since each teacher has a personal and unique approach to students, each interacts with students differently and experiences different aspects of a student's personality. Sharing these experiences provides each faculty member with valuable insight into the possible reasons for a student's behavior and academic performance."

Some faculty report that the learning community altered their relationships with their students and contributed to a more positive classroom atmosphere. "Students are more open and responsive with friends to back them up," one remarked. "Students do qualitatively better; they are more talkative, interested," said another. Another noticed a more cooperative classroom atmosphere: "Students do not perceive themselves as being in competition with one another for grades; in addition the teacher becomes non-threatening." Learn-

ing is an experience shared with students. "I'm having deeper, more enjoyable relationships with students." "Teachers are recognized as participants in a common enterprise—sharing an awareness of a given aspect of our world."

Faculty also appreciate the relationships they form with colleagues. "It's nice to talk with other faculty about the same students, to gain insight into what they learn." Beyond that shared experience, they also find it "invigorating" to think across disciplines, "to discuss content in a deeper, more nuanced way," "to have the opportunity to be creative across disciplines," and "to come up with ideas that encompass more than one field." Working closely with colleagues not only encourages interdisciplinary thinking but also encourages fresh perspectives on one's own discipline: "I'm beginning to understand how other disciplines perceive mine," reported one faculty member. "Thinking about my discipline in relation to others enriches my teaching," said another. New connections and insights with implications for their research projects emerged as well.

Teaching in a learning community also encourages the improvement of teaching. Many faculty members referred to the new ideas and strategies that they learned from colleagues in their learning community. That is another source of renewal: "Trying new teaching techniques that you learn from other learning community faculty is wonderful." The bond the learning community creates among faculty helps them to take risks in their teaching, to try out new things, to have "thoughtful conversations" about ideas and teaching methods that are otherwise rare.

Major Disadvantages for Faculty

Despite having many positive experiences and seeing real advantages for students in a learning community, many faculty expressed concerns about participating in a learning community in the future. Not surprisingly, the time and effort required and the impact of other responsibilities were often cited as disincentives to continued participation. This comment is typical: "Teaching in a learning community means not allowing enough time for research and tenure-granting activities.

It can be tempting to get caught up in activities with students that can be too time-consuming." And although knowing one's students better and gaining insight into their lives is important, such knowledge does not always make one's life easier. As several faculty relate, "the realities of the freshman experience can be painful"; "one sees and feels students' problems more acutely, which can be painful. One has to be careful not to try to solve problems beyond one's scope!" Some faculty expressed concern about the learning community model as a cure-all. "The learning community structure," one respondent notes, "is likely to promise more than it delivers, ultimately leading to frustration and a need to blame oneself or one's students. To do it right puts a real strain on your workload."

Faculty also experienced problems with community development. Sometimes community does not develop; and when it does, it is not always positive. As one faculty member observed, "I have taught learning community classes in which the community reinforced positive student traits—studying, peer editing, and so on. However, I have also taught learning community classes in which the community reinforced negative traits—cheating, rudeness in class, cutting class, and so on. It all depends on the character of the students who wind up in the learning community. How can faculty influence students so peer pressure is toward positive traits?"

Some faculty found work with their colleagues more difficult than anticipated. Personalities clash, "your teaching methods and content are under the microscope for your faculty peers to observe and critique, which can be intimidating at first," and "cooperation can be difficult to achieve." Learning a new way of doing things can also be extraordinarily time consuming.

Despite their reservations, however, most of the respondents did find the experience of teaching in a learning community sufficiently rewarding so that they will do it again. One went so far as to say, "I'd love to be in a permanent community of faculty members who take on a new group of students each year."

Suggestions and Cautions

Consider the broad context. A number of powerful and probably irreversible forces—primarily student need, the research stemming from cognitive science, information technology, and the influence of business concepts like Total Quality Management and learning organizations—are shifting instruction in higher education toward a focus on process and active, collaborative learning. Student need is expressed both in terms of the skills, attributes, talents, and expectations first-year students bring with them to the academy and in terms of those they will need when they leave in order to navigate a changing work environment, to serve effectively as citizens, and to have fulfilling personal lives. Various forms of student-centered learning, including the learning community model, service learning and other experiential learning strategies, the use of information technology for distance, individualized and modular learning, the quality movement, and assessment are all topics on the national agenda as we struggle to reshape higher education.

Central to each topic is the nature of faculty work—how we train for it, how we reward it, how we support and nurture it. Critics outside the academy are less shy than those within in calling for a change in the nature of faculty work to create an educational model effective in meeting the needs of tomorrow's students. Although they may be right, or partially so, those critics all too often demonstrate little understanding of what may be lost as well as what can be gained, of what faculty actually do versus what they need to do in order for the desired changes to occur. Those who want to attract faculty to new models of teaching and learning must confront the issue of faculty roles, rewards, and responsibilities on their campus as, for example, Syracuse University has done in becoming a learning-centered research university.

> "I'd love to be in a permanent community of faculty members who take on a new group of students each year."

Clarify learning community goals. Intuitively learning communities seem like such a good idea for students that they are hard to resist. Any learning community exists, however, in service to a particular set of goals. Claims have been made and variously substantiated for the effectiveness of the learning community in fostering students' involvement in learning and increasing their quality of effort, of providing coherence in the curriculum, and of easing the new students' transition to higher education. The kind of learning community that promotes student learning and persistence is also the most difficult to construct and sustain. Learning communities require the following: small class size, a peer group engaged in common academic purposes, curricular coherence, teaching strategies to foster active and collaborative learning, efforts to promote metacognition, faculty-student interaction, and ongoing assessment.

While overly ambitious changes may promote failure, naive belief in the power of the structure alone will yield few positive results. The learning community is a flexible structure, but the view that major transformations in learning occur simply by enrolling cohorts of students in several classes in common is probably overly optimistic. Without direction and support, students are unlikely to form study groups, to perceive curriculum coherence, or to become more involved. A clear understanding of goals and objectives allows for an accurate assessment of the outcomes of learning communities.

> Without direction and support, students are unlikely to form study groups, to perceive curriculum coherence, or to become more involved.

Build in assessment. Assessing the effectiveness of a given learning community model in the context of a particular campus and student body is essential for improving practice and ensuring continued administrative and faculty support. While most assessments of programs at single institutions suggest that course completion rates and retention are both improved for students in learning communities as compared with those in regular classes, less evidence exists for broader claims such as the amount or depth of student learning, an increased ability to make connections among

disciplines, or participation in study groups in other courses. Often no attempt is made to measure such effects. But as programs increasingly compete for scarce resources, more and more funding decisions are based on the data.

Provide an administrative home. Like all educational innovations, learning communities need administrative support with sufficient resource allocation to sustain the goals of the program over time. Someone other than teaching faculty should handle administrative processes, recruit and orient new faculty participants, assess the program's effectiveness, and be responsible for the ongoing vitality of the program. Too many faculty report that they had to become mini-registrars for their learning community to ensure that students were registered properly and that classrooms and meeting times were scheduled appropriately. Many also assumed responsibility for publicizing and recruiting for the learning community. Most faculty respondents to the questionnaire indicated that the additional time spent developing coherence in the curriculum or working with colleagues and students was time well spent; coping with the administrative details, on the other hand, was a waste of time that discouraged their further participation.

Incorporate successful practices. Many practices increase the likelihood of a learning community's achieving its goals, particularly for first-year students.

1. Include a trained upperclass student mentor or a "near peer," possibly as a co-instructor in a linking seminar or in some Supplemental Instruction role (Martin, Arendale, & Associates, 1993).

2. Provide faculty development and ongoing faculty support. Structure regular meetings; offer coffee and conversation; provide occasions for collaboration.

3. Emphasize active learning strategies. A decade and more of research on how people learn

has only served to reinforce the importance to student learning of the "Seven Principles of Good Practice" outlined by Chickering and Gamson (1987).

4. Allow time for process. As Howard Gardner once said, "the greatest enemy to learning is coverage." If a learning community is to succeed, time must be spent on developing skills in group dynamics. Time is necessary, too, for reflection, to foster the habit of understanding what and how one is learning, for metacognition.

5. Consider using the freshman seminar or a basic writing course as the link to form a learning community. Causing the least disruption to typical curricular structures and teaching assignments, these combinations have worked well on many campuses.

6. Build in classroom assessment. Using the various strategies suggested by Angelo and Cross (1993), classroom assessment enables faculty to understand exactly what and how students are learning on a regular basis, vital information to share within the learning community.

7. Feature an event. Many faculty and students relate that their learning community really began to work when all members of the community did something together—attended a concert or theater performance on campus followed by dinner and discussion, participated in a community service project, made a site visit related to the theme of the course, or completed a "ropes" course or other team-building activity together.

8. Use information technology. Virtual communities can support the physical community through class listservs, web pages, chat rooms for study sessions and discussions (see, for examples, Creed, 1997a, 1997b). These resources are particularly important when learning communities have commuting or working students as members.

9. Plan ahead. A surprising number of faculty respondents to the questionnaire reported be-

ing enlisted to teach in a learning community within a few weeks or even days of the beginning of the semester. A new learning community requires a considerable amount of time for establishing relationships among the instructors and for planning the courses and activities. A lead time of at least a semester and preferably longer is essential.

10. Anticipate problems. As one faculty member reported, "because we got to know our students, we could identify those struggling very early. Unfortunately, we had no idea what to do about it and no one seemed able to tell us." Faculty members shifting from a large lecture for upperclass students to a first-year learning community need to be forewarned that their relationship with students will change. They need to be alerted to the new problems they are likely to encounter, the support services and other resources available to students on campus, and the ways in which their students can gain access to them.

This different relationship and what it implies for faculty and students alike are summarized by one faculty respondent to the questionnaire. Referring to his experience of teaching in a learning community within a residence hall, he writes:

"A typical faculty member in a large class would rarely follow up aggressively on students who have apparently chosen to fail. But the four students in my class who have done no or very little work during the first month of classes are sending a clear signal: I'm in trouble. It can be compared to suicide. They are committing academic suicide. They labor under the false assumption that they cannot make it in college and, therefore, will not try. Or they think they can do nothing and still survive. Both are dangerous roads. The fact that the ten faculty here "living" next to the students (our offices are in one dorm wing), are struggling to find out what makes this generation of students tick says that we go the extra mile. That mile is defined in more than traditional academic terms. We routinely pick up the phone and call our students down to our offices, join them for coffee or organize lunch or dinner get-togethers. We get close to the students in order to discover how they can be better learners. We are interested in affecting the entire development of our students. The old, single class model just is not working for too many, probably the majority of our students. In my 26 years of teaching from one class to another, I always felt something was missing. I now know what that was: The classroom is not a sufficient base from which to affect significant growth."

Rare are the first-year students who do not need confirmation that they can succeed in college, that they can make both friends and good grades, that they can connect what they already know to new fields of study and new ways of knowing and grow intellectually, that they can gain the self-confidence, self-knowledge, and skills so that their learning will continue for a lifetime. Vincent Tinto (1997) reminds us that "at its core college is an educational experience," and it is likely that both our choices of curriculum structure and pedagogy influence student learning and persistence (p. 620). The evidence is strong that the learning community coupled with student-centered teaching strategies can be a transformational tool to foster the learning.

References

Angelo, T. A. (1993, April). A "teacher's dozen": Fourteen research-based principles for improving higher learning in our classrooms. *AAHE Bulletin, 13*, 3-7.

Angelo, T. A., & Cross, K. P. (1993). *Classroom assessment techniques: A handbook for college teachers*. San Francisco: Jossey-Bass.

Astin, A. W. (1993). *What matters in college?* San Francisco: Jossey-Bass.

Chickering, A. W., & Gamson, Z. F. (1987, March). Seven principles for good practice. *AAHE Bulletin, 39*, 3-7.

Creed, T. (1997a). A virtual communal space. *The National Teaching and Learning Forum, 6*(5), 5-6.

Creed, T. (1997b). Choosing a virtual communal space for your course. *The National Teaching and Learning Forum, 7*(1), 3-5.

Ewell, P. T. (1997). *Organizing for learning: A point of entry*. National Center for Higher Education Management Systems (NCHEMS). Draft prepared for discussion at the 1997 AAHE Summer Academy at Snowbird.

Gabelnick, F., MacGregor, J., Matthews, R., & Smith, B. (1990). Learning communities: Creating connections among students, faculty, and disciplines. *New Directions for Teaching and Learning, 41*. San Francisco: Jossey-Bass.

Gose, B. (1998, January 16). More freshmen than ever appear disengaged from their studies, survey finds. *The Chronicle of Higher Education*, A 37.

Learning community programs in Washington. (1995, Spring). *Washington Center News*, 22-29.

MacGregor, J., Matthews, R., Smith, B. L., & Gabelnick, F., (1998, January). *Learning community models*. Unpublished presentation. University of Miami.

Martin, D. C., Arendale, D. R., & Associates. (1993). *Supplemental Instruction: Improving first-year student success in high risk courses* (Monograph No. 7). Columbia, SC: University of South Carolina, National Resource Center for The Freshman Year Experience.

Pascarella, E. T., & Terenzini, P. T. (1991). *How college affects students*. San Francisco: Jossey-Bass.

Rendón, L. I. (1996, November/December). Life on the border. *About Campus*, 14-20.

Tinto, V. (1997). Classrooms as communities: Exploring the educational character of student persistence. *Journal of Higher Education, 68*(6), 599-623.

Tinto, V. (1994). *Building learning communities for new college students*. University Park, PA:

National Center on Postsecondary Teaching, Learning, and Assessment.

Tinto, V., & Goodsell, A. (1993). Freshman interest groups and the first-year experience: Constructing student communities in a large university. *Journal of The Freshman Year Experience, 6*(1), 7-28.

Tinto, V., Goodsell Love, A., & Russo, P. (1993). Building community. *Liberal Education, 79*(4), 16-21.

What research says about improving undergraduate education: Twelve attributes of good practice. (1996, April). *AAHE Bulletin, 48*(8), 5-8.

CHAPTER SIX

Faculty Development In Learning Communities:
The Role of Reflection and Reframing

Scott E. Evenbeck, Barbara Jackson, and John McGrew

Participation in learning communities is emerging as a powerful form of faculty, staff, and student development. Many institutions, in moving from a focus on teaching to a focus on learning, have found that faculty, staff, and student participation in developing and offering learning communities has resulted in important new understandings of students, of their strengths, of how we best serve them, and of how persons can work together across departments.

Learning communities provide a context for faculty and students to focus on student learning. Parker Palmer (1998) argues that the focus of teaching and learning should be faculty and students together approaching the subject in a way that engages students in learning. However, the move from teaching to learning is not enough. The collaborative work and interdisciplinary conversations engendered by learning community participation establishes the ideal context for a shift in focus to the learning itself—the real "point," after all, of teaching and learning. In learning communities, by definition, people are working together across disciplines and roles to support student learning. By making teaching "public" work (Boyer, 1990), faculty and other members of the academic community participate in very powerful professional development in a context of reframing and reflection. This development is not a program offered to faculty, nor a lecture or workshop designed to serve them. Rather, it is the sort of professional practice that Schön (1983) sees as characteristic of professionals in general. In the learning community, faculty do not work in isolation, following long-standing modes of behavior, but rather they engage with other faculty and students, and often with staff members, in transforming the nature of their work.

Context

On many campuses, the majority of students in higher education are not residential, traditional-aged students, enrolled full-time in their academic pursuits. By all standards, the student body is increasingly diverse. Urban, public universities find themselves at the forefront in developing programs to serve this diverse population of students. One such urban university is Indiana University Purdue University Indianapolis (IUPUI). Students on this campus are representative of the students now enrolling in higher education. They are often first-generation college students; they work; they have family obligations; and they represent a wide range of ages, socioeconomic status, and ethnicity.

Like many students entering American educational institutions today, IUPUI students are often underprepared in foundational areas (e.g., reading, writing, and mathematics). At the IUPUI campus where all new students take placement tests in these areas, over 80% of entering students are required to complete developmental courses. Most of the coursework for entering students is in these foundational skills areas in which instruction is not delivered by full-time, tenure-track faculty. Other course placements (Adelman's "empirical" general education, 1995) typically include physical education activity and military science courses that do not require prerequisites. Enrollment in remedial courses does not satisfy general education requirements or provide introduction to courses in a major, but rather is a required prerequisite for "real" college curricula. The systematic exclusion of students on many campuses from the "normal" first-year introductory courses in the disciplines has insulated students taking remedial courses from the faculty and vice versa. Learning communities, consisting of a new first-year seminar course linked to an introductory discipline-based course, have proven to be beneficial to students (Borden & Rooney, 1998; Evenbeck & Foster, 1996; Evenbeck & Williams, 1998).

As is the case at many institutions, the development of learning communities at IUPUI was faculty driven and centered on a one-credit, first-year seminar. The full-time faculty who developed the learning communities worked together to formulate strategies to involve students in a collegial fashion. In the context of "on-the-job training," these faculty borrowed successful strategies from other institutions and then adapted and tailored them to fit the unique needs of IUPUI, the state's only metropolitan university. Following the University of South Carolina model, the first-year seminar includes a common set of curricular and pedagogical requirements. Building on national student-success data, that identifies the quality and extent of social connections as critical to student success, the learning communities at IUPUI have made the establishment of connections to the resources, people, skills, and values of the university community a fundamental goal. Since the faculty member who teaches the first-year seminar also teaches a linked disciplinary course, students have a real "laboratory" in which to apply concepts presented in the seminar.

The learning communities have been designed to build involvement and to stress collaboration across disciplines and across roles. To accomplish that goal, the first-year seminar employs instructional teams to plan and present each section of the course. Resident faculty serve as team anchors, supported in a collaborative teaching effort by a librarian, an academic advisor, a student mentor, and a technology specialist. Faculty and staff must step out of traditional departmental roles to work in a collaborative and reflective fashion developing courses and programs to serve students better. Instructional teams operating collectively have shaped the seminar's philosophy as well as the content and pedagogies, and they have provided a grassroots, as opposed to a top-down, approach to program development.

Faculty Development in
Learning Communities

For most faculty, involvement in a learning community represents a significant change in the conduct of their professional responsibilities. In order to recruit and retain outstanding resident faculty to participate in these initiatives and to sustain their commitment, attention to faculty rewards is an essential feature of the development and administration of learning communities. From the outset, attempts have been made to ensure that faculty receive appropriate recognition for their contributions. Often, these rewards have been conceived of in a very traditional (and somewhat limited) way. Typically, they are identified in terms of the obvious tangible elements—reductions in teaching load assignment, compensation in the form of merit raise increments, and supplemental support for standard professional needs such as summer stipends, research assistance, computers, and travel.

The conception of faculty rewards must, however, become more comprehensive. Since participating faculty consistently assert that the experience of teaching in learning communities is personally rewarding and contributes to professional growth, faculty development itself must be defined as both an unanticipated *individual* reward and a beneficial *institutional* outcome. These personal and professional benefits include improvement in regular teaching assignments and greater articulation within the broader university community. Such benefits are important complements to traditional faculty rewards and incentives.

Faculty Development Outcomes

Many of the outcomes described by faculty in learning communities fit quite comfortably with standard conceptions of faculty development, which emphasize the solitary faculty member's pursuit of new knowledge and skills directly related to his or her professional discipline and acquired through independent activity. These traditional faculty development outcomes include the general improvement in pedagogical strategies applied to regular departmental courses and the garnering of new perspectives or greater depth of knowledge within the person's discipline.

For some faculty, the learning community teaching experience results in enhanced status within the department and among colleagues, especially where innovation in teaching is a valued part of the tenure and/or promotion decisions. Opportunities to conduct research and develop presentations and publications as a result of learning community work likewise fit with traditional notions of faculty development.

All of these are important components to articulate and encourage in an intentional program of faculty development. Many of the faculty development outcomes in learning communities are,

... faculty development itself must be defined as both an unanticipated individual reward and a beneficial institutional outcome.

however, transformative. They go beyond enhancement of traditional faculty roles. Faculty learn to negotiate their traditional environment in new ways because they have developed new understandings and new insights into teaching the new university student. The transformative power of the learning community is perhaps the most unexpected and exciting outcome of all.

Transformative Faculty Development Outcomes

Truly collaborative work on teaching. Participation in learning communities makes it necessary for faculty to work with others in the planning and presentation of courses. Such collaboration provides faculty with the challenge of developing intentional strategies of collaboration. With few notable exceptions for faculty who have taught in interdisciplinary programs, most faculty experiences with and understandings of collaborative work have been limited to that of team teaching. Some faculty are involved in the coordination of multiple sections of introductory courses, while a limited number of faculty have experience as co-lecturers in their disciplines. The prevailing traditional model in most such cases is, however, cooperation, and not genuine collaboration, with faculty still retaining autonomy and control over their section or segment of the course.

The collaboration in learning communities, as seen in the instructional team model described above, is by nature interdependent. Faculty must work in concert with each other and with staff to plan course topics, assignments, pedagogical strategies, and division of labor. Faculty not only must find ways of incorporating into the course design the expanded knowledge base of other faculty and staff such as counselors, librarians, and technologists, but also they are challenged to incorporate the varying perspectives that their partners contribute on appropriate pedagogies to enhance student motivations and abilities. Collaborative work often does not happen naturally or easily for participants. It is labor intensive, involves logistics and coordination, and may provide some uncomfortable challenges to what faculty regard as an effective approach to students, grounded in disciplinary expertise.

Collaboration in the team setting provides the bridge for faculty to a more collaborative classroom environment—one in which students as well as the instructor(s) are active participants in course learning. On the IUPUI campus, for example, many instructional teams for the First-Year Experience seminar do not finalize the syllabus until after students have had the opportunity to express priorities for some of the optional elements. For many faculty, the learning community provides the opportunity to experiment with collaborative and active approaches to classroom learning—an opportunity which would not routinely occur in the context of their regular teaching assignments.

Increased knowledge and use of campus resources. All faculty report increased understanding of the campus as a direct, tangible, and highly useful benefit of their participation in the learning community. As is the case on most campuses, IUPUI is not only highly compartmentalized for students but has been so for many faculty. Many resources that support new students and faculty teaching efforts are either invisible or underutilized. These include such things as health and mental health services, internship and work opportunities, career counseling, programs that support the use of technology in teaching, aspects of information retrieval and resources, and information about advising, registration, and financial aid. Faculty report that their new familiarity with university resources has transferred to their other teaching assignments.

Enhanced collegiality among faculty. The challenge of developing learning communities creates a new sense of collegiality among faculty. The IUPUI campus uses "pods" (regular informal sessions of participating faculty), task-focused committee work related to learning communities, and presentations to university and national audiences to increase both the opportunity and motivation for collegial conversations and interactions, especially across departmental and school lines.

Movement toward an interdisciplinary perspective. A reported outcome of collaboration with faculty colleagues from other academic units is the movement from a uni-disciplinary to a more multi-disciplined perspective. Taking a comprehensive approach to student learning (rather than centering it on the viewpoint of a specific discipline) and working with colleagues from other disciplines encourages faculty to see their discipline in the context of others, to appreciate a given discipline as an integral part of a total university environment.

Creation of a comprehensive professional community focused on new students. The development of learning communities often makes real the claim that it literally "takes a village" to educate a student. The curriculum of a learning community helps ensure that faculty connect across many segments of the university and form such a community. Learning communities for new students may also forge connections among individuals and units controlling the resources that are key to academic success for new students. Faculty are enthusiastic about the collaborative nature of learning communities not only because of their obvious benefit to student academic success but also because of personal benefits such as professional development and broadening peer networks.

These individual connections among faculty, staff, and administrators in learning communities result in the development of an increased mutual understanding of roles. Faculty feel their colleagues have a better understanding and a greater respect for the nature and demands of faculty work. In turn, faculty gain a better understanding of the roles of other campus professionals, a respect for their capabilities, and an appreciation of their unique constraints and pressures. The faculty are making their own work "public work," and they carry out their activities in a context

> Learning community faculty understand that they must convince students of the importance of critical thinking by beginning with things that are important to the student.

where others are also making their work public—not working in isolation.

Creation of student-centered learning environments. Involvement in the learning community lays the groundwork for faculty to move from teaching in isolation, focused on a one-way transfer of information, toward an approach that is centered on student learning and subject mastery. Faculty who adopt this shift in focus may take on the role of "mentor." This expanded role gives faculty valuable insights into the perceptions of the students. Faculty may be depressed or frustrated by the fact that students sometimes demonstrate little in the way of intellectual motivation. University work may be a low priority in the spectrum of students' life commitments, and they may be underprepared for university study. Yet faculty report that they learn to teach where students are—rather than where they're assumed to be. Learning community faculty understand that they must convince students of the importance of critical thinking by beginning with things that are important to the student. Faculty learn how to explain such values as academic honesty and diversity, so that students understand why these are valued; faculty also learn how to demonstrate at personal levels why study skills and strategies that worked in high school often are inadequate and inappropriate at the university.

Faculty development often includes occasions in which faculty themselves learn to "reframe" or take a different perspective on a problem. The term "reframing" comes from therapeutic literature, referring to the search for new or alternate perspectives when traditional problem-solving methods fail. For example, "acting out" may be reframed as a child's attempt to gain needed attention from a parent. Learning community faculty are also invited to take a different perspective (i.e., the student or the university's perspective) from the one they adopt in other teaching contexts. While learning community courses clearly have course-content goals akin to those of other courses, a marked difference exists in the emphasis on extra-course goals. A focus on extra-course goals reframes the role of the instructor from a lecturer who transmits knowledge to one who is an agent for student success. The reframing of the instructor role places instructors in an unfamiliar position that demands a new approach to teaching. They begin to focus on student learning rather than subject-matter teaching. This new focus on student learning includes attention to students' cognitive and social development, both in and outside the classroom. Palmer (1998) suggests that this new focus leads to the change of perspective outlined below:

- From the role of evaluator (distant, objective) to the role of coach (how I can help this student succeed, both in the learning community courses and in other courses)

- From lecturer (medium of knowledge) to collaborator (what we can do to ensure student learning)

- From "assigner/grader" (setting goals for students) to support person (what does the student need in order to learn)

- From individual responsibility to shared responsibility

- From needs of the course or department to needs of the university

- From teaching as a solo act to teaching as a team

- From focus on the student as knowledgeable/competent in a narrow area to focus on the student as a whole person

- From focus on the student in the classroom to focus on the person in context

One of the benefits of reframing is that faculty often adopt a learning- or student-centered approach in the courses they teach outside the learning community. Faculty members may begin to view themselves differently: as members of the university, not just as members of a department; as support persons in learning rather than as merely lecturers; as members of a multi-disciplinary learning community, rather than as solitary teachers. Certainly, it is possible that the experience may lead to new perspectives on the self, on other faculty (especially in departments involved in the learning communities or in the typical curriculum of first-year students), on staff, on students, and on pedagogy.

Intentional reflection on how one teaches makes reframing possible. Such reframing often occurs when faculty work together to plan, implement, and assess the learning communities. At IUPUI, for example, faculty meet in "pods" to share insights with one another. In addition, academic advisors, librarians, and student mentors must meet with each other as well as with faculty to share insights and reflect on the learning communities. For professionals gaining new insight into their work, "reflection-in-action" becomes a very powerful process (Schön, 1983). The program at IUPUI institutionalizes this reflection-in-action so that the professional working across and within role boundaries reflects on his or her service to students and then works with other professionals to "test" and extend strategies for serving entering students. Despite the efficacy of such reflection, one caution remains: ". . . our enthusiasm for reflection can be converted exclusively into a concern for technique" (Brookfield, 1995, p. 216).

Paradigms For Faculty Development

Learning communities thus present themselves as outstanding venues for faculty development. Learning communities, by their very nature, mandate collaborative work. They are an excellent vehicle for implementing the critical elements educators are endorsing as appropriate for contemporary higher education. The learning communities program for students can serve as a real "learning community" for the faculty and other instructional team members as well. Learning communities for entering students provide the arena where the transitions in faculty roles and academic culture can occur in universities in the next century (Rice, 1991). These transitions include movement from a faculty-centered university to a more student- and community-responsive institution. Learning communities change highly individualistic ways of working (my work) to collaboration and engagement (our work) and change the passive learning of unexamined assumptions to active learning and a culture of evi-

dence. Learning communities facilitate democratic participation rather than elitism.

Assuming that these sorts of transitions are essential for the viability of undergraduate education, the following strategies for faculty development initiatives linked to learning communities are recommended. These suggested features and processes are affirmed by our actual experiences at IUPUI, and are captured by the concept of the "reflective practitioner" (Schön, 1983). By encouraging faculty involved in learning communities to become reflective practitioners, the following behaviors become habitual:

- *Intentional development of a personal philosophy of teaching.* An integral component of faculty development is the opportunity to reflect, develop, and articulate one's own understanding of teaching and learning. Faculty development programs should encourage the examination of individual teaching strategies and foster approaches that reach beyond the boundaries of traditional discipline-based scholarship, service, and teaching. As faculty identify their own teaching philosophies, they may become more cognizant of their proficiency in reaching the nontraditional undergraduate students who represent diverse levels of preparedness and readiness for college.

- *A holistic and contextual approach to students.* Students become more engaged in learning activities that make direct connections to the realities of their daily lives. Faculty development opportunities can provide faculty with the skills to enhance conceptual thinking and pedagogical strategies to help students make connections between in-class learning and out-of-class activities, between cognitive development and social development.

- *Self-reflection.* Programs of faculty development focused on pedagogy must learn to include (along with skills and discipline knowledge enhancement) opportunities for self-reflection so that faculty may examine their own conscious or subconscious biases about students, curriculum content, new teaching strategies, communication patterns, and interactional styles.

- *Development of skills in interpersonal relationships and group dynamics.* The establishment of a mutually supportive environment in which students feel safe and comfortable to share their educational successes and failures requires a well-designed and intentional curriculum and the articulation of group-facilitation skills. Faculty development in the learning communities increases faculty skills, leading to a campus climate of collaboration.

Administrative Support for Faculty Development

Faculty development as an outcome of the implementation of learning communities is a highly desirable institutional goal. Support for faculty must include the opportunity to work with persons in other roles on campus, and that support must be within and across disciplines.

The program at IUPUI attended to process—a process of intentionality and reflection by the participants working in collaborative fashion. In this context, the strategy was "place and train" rather than "train and place." There was neither a specific model to replicate nor a prescribed curriculum. While the campus has developed a model and now a statement of student learning outcomes, the stated intention of the program was to operationalize an "experimenting place," a context where faculty and other members of the team were asked to work collaboratively to try things out with continual reflection. Recognizing the uniqueness of the IUPUI campus and its students, faculty and administrators knew that no program could be easily "imported." At IUPUI faculty have been offered and have exercised real decision-making power for development, implementation, and continuing improvement of the learning community program. This ownership provides the foundation for the enhancement of faculty skills and competencies discussed above. It provides an inviting framework for faculty to come together as peers to discuss, develop, and

assess ways of meeting student needs in new and creative ways.

Those responsible for programs must make every effort to provide adequate space, time, technology, and other resources required. These kinds of transformative opportunities require reflection, collaboration, communication, and innovation on the part of faculty and other professionals. Allocation of adequate resources is necessary. Learning communities, particularly if they involve the high degree of intentionality and reflection that optimize their outcomes, cannot be an "add-on" or administrative matter. The intense involvement of faculty is critical. Articulation of faculty development outcomes provides important justification for the allocation of resources. For a more detailed description of the types of resources needed, see Chapter 3.

The purview of faculty development is broad and encompasses virtually all dimensions of faculty work. A wide array of activities, programs, interventions, and occasions, from the formal and highly-structured to the informal and spontaneous, should be encouraged and supported. Faculty are the best positioned to identify activities appropriate to their situation and the institution. Some of the activities at IUPUI that resulted in faculty development outcomes include:

- *Specific task-based activities associated with aspects of program development.* Faculty work in groups or committees to identify successful pedagogical strategies and practices, to develop technology curriculum, to interface with the orientation staff, and to define course goals and common requirements.

- *Occasions for reflection.* In addition to time allocated for course planning and team preparation, it is important to structure occasions for both "brainstorming" and activities that encourage reflection. Examples include planning symposia, assessment and other research associated with the program, and seminar-like groups which prepare presentations and publications. This is the kind of work valued by faculty—often drawing upon their typical strengths.

- *Encouraging the development of mechanisms for individual and mutual support.* Peer mentorships, in which experienced faculty are paired with beginners, and regular informal "help" sessions in which peer support is provided, are especially important to development of self-reflection, intergroup dynamics, and community building.

- *Providing a national context for first-year seminar work.* As important, productive and satisfying as working with one's campus colleagues has proven to be at IUPUI, outside stimuli and the ability to place campus perspectives in a broader context have served to enhance the faculty development out comes. The campus regularly seeks quality outside resources in support of issues identified as critical to the campus.

Faculty development is both an outcome and a reward for participation in a learning community. Faculty encounter opportunities to become more current, effective, and engaged teachers while they participate in positive experiences for professional growth and enhanced collegiality.

Critical to sustaining this effort, which is beneficial for students, the institution, and individual faculty, is a concerted effort to ensure that faculty are rewarded. It is important that outstanding faculty are at the center of the design, delivery, and assessment of learning communities. The university environment mirrors the corporate trend toward increased demands for output without increased compensation. Faculty are asked to teach not only more courses, but better courses, to have exemplary research accomplishments, and to provide escalating amounts of institutional service. The engagement of the most capable faculty in the service of entering students mandates a competitive set of incentives which include tangible and traditional rewards *coupled with* significant professional development opportunities.

References

Adelman, C. (1995). *The new college course map and transcript files: Changes in course-taking and achievement, 1972-1993.* Washington, DC: National Institute of Postsecondary Education, Libraries, and Lifelong Learning. Office of Educational Research and Improvement, U.S. Department of Education.

Borden, V. M. H., & Rooney, P. M. (1998). Evaluating and assessing learning communities. *Metropolitan Universities Journal, 9*(1), 73-88.

Boyer, E. L. (1990). *Scholarship reconsidered: Priorities of the professoriate.* Princeton, NJ: The Carnegie Foundation for the Advancement of Learning.

Brookfield, S. D. (1995). *Becoming a critically reflective teacher.* San Francisco: Jossey-Bass.

Evenbeck, S. E., & Foster, M. C. (1996). *The urban university first-year experience: Building community benefits faculty and other university professionals and serves students well.* Washington, DC: ERIC Clearinghouse on Higher Education. (ERIC Document Reproduction Service No. ED 418 608)

Evenbeck, S. E., & Williams, G. (1998). Learning communities: An instructional team approach. *Metropolitan Universities Journal, 9*(1), 35-46.

Palmer, P. (1998). *The courage to teach: Exploring the inner landscape of a teacher's life.* San Francisco: Jossey-Bass.

Rice, R. E. (1991, Spring). The new American scholar: Scholarship and the purposes of the university. *Metropolitan Universities Journal, 1*(4), 7-18.

Schön, D. A. (1983). *The reflective practitioner: How professionals think in action.* New York: Basic Books.

The authors wish to acknowledge the contributions of Rosalie Vermette, Betty Anderson, Kevin Robbins, and Marie Watkins in a presentation addressing the issue of faculty development, presented at the National Conference on The First Year Experience and Students in Transition, Columbia, SC, February 1998.

CHAPTER SEVEN

Learning Communities:
Partnerships Between Academic and Student Affairs

Charles C. Schroeder, Frankie D. Minor, and Theodore A. Tarkow

A revolution is underway, and we must be willing to join the cause or be swept aside in the inevitable transformations that will occur. No where is this revolution more apparent than in recent calls for reform of higher education (Wingspread Group on Higher Education, 1993; Kellogg Commission on the Future of State and Land-Grant Universities, 1997) that stress the need to connect undergraduate experiences with student learning. To respond to this mandate, institutions must provide the conditions that foster "seamless" learning environments—settings that promote intentional, coherent, integrated, and continuous learning. Well-developed and effective learning communities promote intentional and integrated learning because they represent performance support systems that link and align a variety of institutional resources to ensure high levels of educational attainment. The development of learning communities, however, requires new organizational behaviors on the part of individuals in academic and student affairs leadership positions—systematic and coordinated efforts that marshal and direct resources to accomplish specific learning outcomes. Forging cross-functional, collaborative partnerships to create learning communities also requires risk taking and a willingness to challenge the educational assumptions and organizational boundaries of the institution, as well as a readiness to move beyond traditional roles and "comfort zones."

This chapter describes the importance of collaborative partnerships between academic and student affairs in the design and implementation of learning communities. The first section delineates different definitions of learning communities and explores why collaborative partnerships are essential for their development. A review of obstacles and constraints to collaboration is then explained, followed by a case example that illustrates an effective partnership. The next section describes strategies for building effective partnerships. The chapter concludes with additional recommendations for creating, nurturing, and sustaining partnerships.

Collaborative Partnerships: An Essential Element in the Development of Learning Communities

In their compelling essay, "Living with Myths: Undergraduate Education in America," Terenzini and Pascarella (1994) posed a major challenge for educators committed to the reform of undergraduate education:

> Organizationally and operationally, we have lost sight of the forest. If undergraduate education is to be enhanced, faculty members, joined by academic and student affairs administrators, must devise ways to deliver undergraduate education that are as comprehensive and integrated as the ways that students actually learn. A whole new mindset is needed to capitalize on the interrelatedness of the in- and out-of-class influences on student learning and the functional interconnectedness of academic and student affairs divisions. (p. 32)

Learning communities provide an excellent venue for addressing this challenge because they can enhance the degree of integration and coherence among various disciplines and co-curricular experiences. Their development, however, requires authentic, cross-functional partnerships between individuals in academic and student affairs.

To be successful, collaborative partnerships between academic and student affairs must be developed from a common reference point—a mutually agreed upon definition of learning communities. Gabelnick, MacGregor, Matthews, and Smith (1990) suggest a fairly traditional definition of learning communities as ". . . curricular structures that link different disciplines around a common theme or question. They give greater coherence to the curriculum and provide students and faculty with a vital sense of shared inquiry" (p. 6). The emphasis of this definition on curricular structures and student-faculty interaction fails to capitalize on what we have learned from over 50 years of research on college impact—that cognitive and affective development are inextricably intertwined and that the curriculum and out-of-class activities are not discreet, independent variables, but rather affect one another in often profound ways

(Pascarella & Terenzini, 1991). Furthermore, the Gabelnick et al. (1990) definition does not suggest the need for collaboration between academic and student affairs simply because of the exclusive focus on the relationship between curricular structures and different disciplines. This definition also fails to capitalize on the importance of a variety of student interactions in the educational process in multiple settings both on and off campus.

Astin (1985) offers a broader, more encompassing definition of learning communities as, "small subgroups of students . . . characterized by a common sense of purpose . . . that can be used to build a sense of group identity, cohesiveness and uniqueness that encourages continuity and the integration of diverse curricular and co-curricular experiences" (p. 161). While Gabelnick et al. (1990) emphasize the thematic linking of traditional disciplines, Astin focuses primarily on student interactions that integrate both curricular and co-curricular experiences; the former stresses structure, the latter function.

A definition that manifests a rapprochement between these two themes provides a compelling framework and reference point necessary for creating partnerships between academic and student affairs to design effective learning communities. This definition describes learning communities as ". . . characterized by associational groups of students and teachers, sharing common values and a common understanding of purpose, interacting within a context of curricular and co-curricular structures and functions that link traditional disciplines and co-curricular experiences in the vital pursuit of shared inquiry" (Schroeder & Hurst, 1996, p. 178). This definition responds to the challenge posed by Terenzini and Pascarella (1994) by demonstrating that learning communities can be seamless learning environments that capitalize on the interrelatedness of the in- and out-of-class influences on student learning and the interconnectedness of academic and student affairs functions. The development of purposeful and powerful learning communities, therefore, can only be realized through cross-functional, collaborative partnerships (Bloland, Stamatakos, & Rogers, 1996). Although collaboration has been an espoused value within the academy for decades, in reality a variety of obstacles and constraints have made partnerships between academic affairs and student affairs difficult to achieve and even harder to maintain.

Obstacles and Constraints to Developing Effective Partnerships

During the past 30 years, college and university enrollments have more than quadrupled. As institutions have become more complex, we have attempted to address complexities through specialization, and in the process our organizations have become increasingly fragmented. Today many campuses—especially large public universities—are characterized not by a sense of community, but rather by a constellation of independent principalities and fiefdoms, each disconnected from the others and from any common institutional purpose or transcending values. On these and other campuses, for example, student affairs divisions, colleges, and schools are often quite autonomous, with different foci, priorities, and expectations for staff, faculty, and students. Conditions such as these often exacerbate the traditional and persistent gap that has existed between academic affairs and student affairs for decades. As Blake (1979) states, "People in student affairs, knowing that education is, after all, the mission of the institution, justify their activities as educational. But the more they do this, the less often they convince their faculty colleagues. A persistent gap seems to exist between the two groups of people on campus who work most closely with students" (p. 280).

On most campuses, collaboration between academic affairs and student affairs is certainly more the exception rather than the rule. Or, when it does occur, it often reflects a superficial quality, such as faculty being invited to share a meal with residence hall staff and students. One might ask, "What prevents collaboration between the two groups on campus most directly involved with students?" Although responses to this question

> As institutions have become more complex, we have attempted to address complexities through specialization, and in the process our organizations have become increasingly fragmented.

vary by institution, a number of major factors can inhibit collaboration. First, there appears to be a consistent lack of understanding and appreciation for the unique and distinctive roles of student affairs and academic affairs in higher education. Blake (1996) has suggested some fundamental cultural differences between faculty and student affairs educators in terms of their personality styles, educational preparation, values, and purposes. For example, for decades the formal curriculum has been separated from the informal co-curriculum. As a result, many student affairs staff, as well as most faculty, view teaching and learning to be the primary responsibility of the faculty. From this perspective, the role of student affairs becomes ancillary, supplementary, or complementary to the academic mission of the institution.

Whitt (1996) suggests that student affairs educators reinforce separation between in-class and out-of-class learning because they are primarily uncomfortable initiating partnerships with academic colleagues for a variety of reasons, including lack of experience communicating across the cultures of the two groups. This "communication gap" results, in part, from basic value differences between faculty and student affairs cultures. Faculty, for example, are often iconoclastic thinkers in their own fields who value creation and dissemination of knowledge and autonomy while student affairs educators value holistic student development and collaboration.

Another factor that can limit collaboration is the rigid and encapsulated organizational roles characteristic of both student affairs and academic affairs. In traditional, hierarchical organizations, specialization has led to increased compartmentalization, often resulting in what has been described as "functional silos" or "mine shafts." These vertical structures, with their well-defined reporting lines, can be effective at promoting interaction *within* functional units, but they limit risk taking and create obstacles to coordination and collaboration *between* units. Staff in student affairs, in particular, have kept their educational efforts focused almost exclusively within their organizational boundaries, rather than reaching out and assuming a broader, institutional perspective essential for collaboration (Garland, 1985). The bureaucratic emphasis on control and stability, rather than on innovation, encourages a sense of predictability and stability, thereby resulting in systems that maintain balance and continuity (Schroeder, Nichols, & Kuh, 1983). Hence, a great reluctance to change established practices exists whether or not the practices are currently working well. Forging collaborative partnerships between academic affairs and student affairs requires overcoming this tyranny of custom. Seymour (1995) alludes to the tyranny of the routine and conventional practices when he states, "Most organizations have shared assumptions that protect the status quo and provide few opportunities for learning. Standard operating procedures can become so institutionalized that competence becomes associated with how well one adheres to the rules" (p. 101).

Finally, well-intentioned efforts to promote collaboration are often derailed because of competing assumptions about what constitutes effective undergraduate learning (Kuh, 1997). The primacy of the curriculum and course work (particularly in the major) are highly valued by faculty while informal learning which usually occurs through out-of-class experiences is prized by student affairs educators. Faculty often focus their efforts on facilitating the cognitive and intellectual development of their students whereas student affairs educators promote affective, psychosocial dimensions of students' personal development. Not surprisingly, students' views of what really matters in undergraduate education are often different from those of faculty and student affairs administrators (Kuh et al., 1994). Clearly, divergent views and assumptions such as these are rooted in different institutional cultures, and these cultural differences must be understood and appreciated if partnerships are to be developed, nurtured, and sustained.

In developing collaborative partnerships between student affairs and academic affairs, it is important to distinguish between the means and the end. Partnerships are a means to a greater end—that end being the implementation of effective learning communities that promote student success. The following case example illustrates how effective partnerships can result in higher levels of student learning and educational attainment.

Freshman Interest Groups (FIGs): A Collaborative Partnership that Works

With the arrival of a new chancellor, the University of Missouri-Columbia (MU), an Association of American Universities (AAU), Carnegie Research I, land grant institution, established a goal to "recapture the public's trust" by focusing more attention on promoting student success through enhancing undergraduate experiences. To respond to this mandate, educational partnerships were forged between the Division of Student Affairs and the College of Arts and Sciences to design residential learning communities that would accomplish the following objectives:

- Substantially enhance academic achievement, retention, and educational attainment for first-year students

- Make the campus "psychologically small" by creating peer reference groups for new students

- Purposely integrate curricular and co-curricular experiences through the development of a seamless learning environment

- Provide a venue for enabling admitted students to register early for their fall classes

- Encourage faculty to integrate ideas, concepts, content, writing, assessment, and research from their various disciplines across the curriculum, thereby enhancing general education outcomes for students

To accomplish these objectives, the university created the Freshman Interest Group (FIG) program which blended elements of similar programs at the universities of Oregon and Washington. The program was initiated with the College of Arts and Sciences because of the college's commitment to enhancing student success in core courses, its receptivity to experimenting with a new educational delivery system, and the support from well-respected, senior faculty members.

The FIG program allows groups of 15-20 first-year students to be enrolled in sections of the same three general education courses, to live in the same residence halls, and to enroll in a one-semester course that attempts to integrate the three general education courses. Each group also participates in discussions on subjects ordinarily covered in "University 101" courses. The program was initially launched in 1995 with 22 communities organized around general academic themes (e.g., Ancient Peoples and Culture, Society and Science, and America's Diversity). By the fall of 1998, the program had been expanded to over 1,000 students enrolled in 60 FIGs that include all of MU's schools and colleges.

Encompassing the spectrum of first-year curricula, FIGs are located in more than two-thirds of the university's 19 residence halls. The program utilizes existing resources and combines them in an intentional, purposeful manner. Blocks of rooms are set aside for each FIG in first-year residence halls. The courses making up a FIG are traditional courses; hence, there are no real direct instructional costs for the program. The majority of the program's costs are associated with funding peer advisors (i.e., juniors or seniors with majors related to the FIG themes) who live with their students in the residence halls and who co-facilitate the pro-seminars with faculty or student affairs staff members. Peer advisors (PAs) are exceptional role models who demonstrate academic excellence (i.e., average 3.7 GPA) and superior interpersonal and communication skills. PAs bear significant responsibility for the FIG's success by serving as the principal agents who connect and integrate all aspects of the program.

Following the initial piloting of a FIG approach to freshman scheduling, a large planning committee—with representatives from academic departments, numerous student affairs offices, and the student community—met to outline year one of the program. Faculty from different departments, together with colleagues from the Learning Center, Admissions and Registration, the General Education Program and the Advisors Forum met weekly, building along the way the first steps of an effective partnership that sought to understand the nature and context of each other's professional culture and traditional work environment. This type of cross-functional collaboration required an understanding of and an appreciation for the perspectives of individuals in the two primary institutional zones—academic and student affairs. From the start, faculty and academic support staff had to become quickly familiar with some of the basic issues confronting colleagues in residence life, such as room assignments, community development issues, program and facility accessibility, roommate matching, and even logistics like opening residence halls and staff training. Student affairs staff became oriented to the realm of academic advising, course scheduling, the complexities of transcript evaluation, and the difficulties of using high school records as a guide for placement. Furthermore, the fact that entering students traditionally received residence hall assignments at one time of the year, but their academic schedules at a different time of the year, posed logistical problems, especially since both academic and student affairs representatives advanced good reasons for maintaining the status quo. And while it was clear that the campus was committed to reforming undergraduate education, MU, like most institutions, wanted as much reform for as little expenditure as possible; therefore, before any central administrative funds could be allocated for the program, both Residence Life and the College of Arts and Sciences had to demonstrate that the FIG program was worthy of institutional support.

Demonstrating their own belief in the value of the FIG program, both Residence Life and the College of Arts and Sciences committed the funding to sponsor the first year of the program. The subsequent analysis of its efficacy (Pike, 1996; Pike, Schroeder, & Berry, 1997) clearly demonstrated that the program deserved institutional support.

Peer advisors bear significant responsibility for the FIG's success by serving as the principal agents who connect and integrate all aspects of the program.

For example, the program had a major impact on first-year student achievement, retention, and learning. FIG participants exhibited significantly higher grades, retention rates, and gains in general education outcomes; they also reported higher levels of academic and social integration and institutional commitment than did other students. They demonstrated higher levels of involvement, faculty-student interaction, and interaction with peers. Perhaps most significantly, the academic and intellectual content of these interactions was significantly higher for FIG students. Because of these impressive results, all subsequent funding of the program was provided by the chancellor, the provost and the vice chancellor for student affairs—a fact that symbolized the importance of the partnership at the highest levels of the institution!

As the program's success continues to grow, and as the benefits of partnerships continue to present themselves to both academic affairs and student affairs colleagues, the planning committee is now addressing expansion of the FIG model to include freshmen not living in the residence halls. The inclusion of this student group will add new colleagues to the emerging partnerships as "virtual FIGs" (via monitored chat rooms) join the ranks and as Greek life colleagues begin working to encourage pledge classes to participate in the program.

The program's success has also contributed indirectly to faculty development initiatives. For example, faculty in some FIGs are now intentionally planning curriculum for their own courses that complement and integrate with the other FIG courses. The healthy relationships that have been forged through these educational partnerships are leading to other learning community initiatives, including the development of two residential colleges—one structured around the theme of civic engagement (leadership and service), the other, natural sciences and mathematics. Another result of the FIG program's success is that it has encour-

> FIG participants exhibited significantly higher grades, retention rates, and gains in general education outcomes; they also reported higher levels of academic and social integration and institutional commitment than did other students.

aged faculty and administrators to work more closely to integrate out-of-class learning experiences with traditional in-class instruction.

Effective Strategies for Building Educational Partnerships

The FIG program at the University of Missouri-Columbia is successful primarily because of a number of specific strategies that were utilized for building effective partnerships between academic affairs and student affairs. This section highlights those strategies and describes their impact on the development and implementation of the FIG program at MU. The strategies include the following:

1. *The first step in developing collaborative partnerships is to identify a common purpose.* For academic and student affairs personnel, it is important to reach a general understanding as to what matters in undergraduate education—what, for example, is important and worth addressing through collaboration? Why should learning communities be created in the first place? How will students, academic faculty, student affairs staff, and the institution benefit? On most campuses, academic affairs and student affairs understand the importance of the following objectives: enhancing academic achievement, retention, and educational attainment for freshmen; making the campus "psychologically small and safe" for new students; and integrating curricular and co-curricular experiences to enhance general education outcomes for freshmen. By reaching consensus on the mutual importance of these objectives, individuals in academic and student affairs can establish the "common ground" for the development of learning communities. This common ground provides the context within which a partnership can be developed and sustained.

The partners in the FIG program at MU define student success as their common purpose, and more specifically, a successful transition from high school to college as a foundation for subsequent success. Faculty and academic administrators who work with first-year students identify common issues and concerns affecting new students. Similarly, residential life and other student affairs staff share their own observations and experiences regarding the needs and concerns of first-year students. The FIG planning team then develops successful strategies to integrate and enhance existing support initiatives and to address gaps or missing links where new students do not encounter the "seamless" experience characteristic of a learning community. This provides the essential "common sense of purpose" required for successful collaboration.

2. *The design of effective freshman learning communities requires joint planning and implementation.* Cross-functional teams, composed of faculty, student affairs administrators, and students bring multiple perspectives to bear on the design of learning communities. Including colleagues in faculty development programs, academic advising, and the learning center—functional units that "straddle" academic and student affairs—can enhance the planning and implementation process. Furthermore, planning teams need to operate at multiple levels. Deans and directors need to be involved, particularly at the policy level, but mid-level managers and teaching faculty make the program work.

MU's primary FIG planning team, a broadly representative group, is essential for creating a truly seamless experience for students; however, it also requires members to compromise on traditional approaches to delivering services to create an integrated learning system. Although a large group is helpful for discussion and policy development, a smaller, core group meets weekly and makes most operational decisions.

3. *A variety of resources—human, fiscal and, in some cases, physical—must be linked to achieve mutually agreed-upon objectives (i.e., improved freshman retention, enhanced academic achievement, etc.).* Hence, partnerships flourish when cross-functional teams agree on desired outcomes and

are willing to allocate the necessary resources to achieve them.

Members of departments and divisions working on the planning team at MU each commit staff time and talents, from academic advisors developing course sequences, to registrars pre-registering students in courses, to residential life staff hand-assigning students outside of the traditional, automated process. Residential life staff become well-versed in course registration and curriculum, while academic staff make residence hall room assignments. Existing support services, such as tutoring and advising, are coordinated and integrated with other initiatives. In perhaps the strongest demonstration of linking resources, both academic and student affairs contribute equal financial resources to support the program.

4. *Collaborative partnerships require individuals in student affairs and academic affairs to coordinate in- and out-of-class learning experiences to achieve desired learning community outcomes.* Well-developed out-of-class experiences complement and reinforce classroom learning. Effective partnerships recognize the value of leadership experiences, internships, field trips, and community service activities in achieving specific learning community outcomes.

Capitalizing on each other's strengths, MU's academic and student affairs staff seek to apply their knowledge and skills in each other's traditional arena. Faculty and academic administrators expect "out of class" experiences to enhance in-class instruction. Student affairs staff assist by utilizing their group development and program-planning skills to help with the formation of cohesive FIGs and to design successful co-curricular programs. An example is a weekend field trip with one FIG (Varieties of Human Experience) wherein all three instructors travel with students to Native American burial mounds outside St. Louis. The religious studies professor discusses the religious significance of the mounds, while the anthropology professor points out the cultural and archeological meaning, and the writing instructor asks the students to integrate their class readings and field experiences into a writing assignment. Other FIGs visit museums relevant to their study (Ancient Peoples and Cultures), view theater presentations (Art and Our Times), attend a lecture by leading professionals like Tom Brokaw (Journalism), perform environmental service (Our Environment), and develop a video (Communication).

5. *Senior administrators in academic affairs and student affairs must be strong champions and advocates for innovation and change; they must make visible their commitments to developing, nurturing, and sustaining partnerships.* Senior administrators who make public statements about the importance of collaboration and the centrality of learning communities to undergraduate education reform underscore the importance of cross-functional dialogue and cooperation. More importantly, they must also demonstrate (model) effective collaboration in their own conduct.

The associate dean for arts and sciences and the director of residential life both present information to prospective students at large recruitment events. Each not only touts the value of the FIGs but also other initiatives in each other's domain with which they have become familiar due to their collaboration. Likewise, communication to students, parents, faculty, even senior institutional leaders comes jointly from the associate dean and director to demonstrate the collaborative partnership that exists. They, along with a variety of other faculty and staff involved with FIGs, are now working on a number of other projects unrelated to FIGs but which seek to create the successful transition to college and seamless learning experience for new students. Similarly, the vice chancellor for student affairs and chancellor both cite the success of the FIG program not only for the students but also for institutional effectiveness in their reports to other senior administrators, alumni, curators, and state legislators.

6. *Educational partners from academic and student affairs must carefully define desired outcomes and develop assessment strategies to evaluate the impact of their learning communities.* Jointly determined assessment tasks and data-driven tools produce critical information of interest to both staff and faculty in student and academic affairs while enabling partners to utilize assessment data to continuously improve the quality of their freshman learning communities.

Although anecdotal information is powerfully rewarding, comprehensive assessment data is essential not only to guide effective planning, but also to demonstrate the benefits of the program to others. FIG students have been compared with their non-FIG counterparts and have experienced higher levels of academic achievement, retention, faculty interaction, academic and social integration, and satisfaction. In comparisons to national data on gains in college, FIG students rank above the national average. Assessment data has also been essential in identifying additional personal and financial support for the program, and for recruitment of new participants. In addition to assessing student satisfaction with the program, feedback from parents, an often untapped constituency group, has been solicited as well. In addition to providing viable suggestions and input, this form of assessment serves as a tremendous vehicle for improving the image of both the program and the campus.

7. *Finally, collaborative partnerships require thinking and acting systemically.* Because learning communities are, in fact, performance support systems, they require a systems approach to organizational effectiveness by linking and aligning goals, responsibilities, and resources from academic affairs and student affairs to enhance freshman success.

New approaches to undergraduate education reform—such as the FIG program—require new ways of thinking about traditional programs and services. Although we must continue to enroll students, provide housing for them, advise, register, and teach them, these can no longer be considered independent, discrete experiences. To achieve maximum student success, learning communities must be designed to integrate and connect these often disjointed parts. This invariably will require adjustments to traditional approaches. For example, housing assignments were moved up two months to accommodate this program. However, even for non-participants, this program has increased satisfaction with our process. Likewise, early co-enrollment strategies developed for the FIG program are now being applied or adapted to serve a broader range of students. Furthermore, a new goal is to have all admitted students pre-enrolled in some courses prior to their graduation from high school.

Recommendations for Building and Sustaining Partnerships

Based upon our experience in developing cross-functional partnerships at MU, we feel that the following recommendations and suggestions are worth considering in creating similar partnerships on other campuses throughout the country. Hence, when developing educational partnerships between student affairs and academic affairs, please consider the following:

1. Become an advocate for partnerships by taking the initiative, rather than waiting for opportunities to present themselves. Ask key stakeholders from academic and student affairs to explain their goals and current initiatives designed to help students learn, develop and succeed; find out what challenges they face in trying to meet those goals. Look for ways to utilize learning communities as venues for helping them achieve their goals that are consistent with or that can be integrated with goals within your program and resources at your disposal. Seek out connections, common threads, or "win-win" opportunities.

2. Identify the obstacles that students face in the delivery of academic or student support services that inhibit their learning or success (e.g., isolation, randomness of individual experiences, disjointed attempts at delivery of essential support services). Initial efforts at collaboration should be approached on a pilot basis and focused on issues that are reasonably correctable. Try to avoid political mine fields on your first attempt, and don't bite off more than you can chew.

3. Identify faculty and academic and student affairs administrators who have the appropriate combination of authority and resources and have demonstrated a commitment to student success or adaptability to change. Look for faculty who have won teaching awards or other student recognition honors. At Carnegie Research I institutions like the University of Missouri, tenured faculty are more likely to participate in innovative programming than are junior faculty. Often junior faculty must be more concerned about gaining tenure and may see these initiatives as ancillary to their central purpose (i.e., tenure). On many other campuses, junior faculty are eager to participate in learning communities because they have an opportunity to collaborate with veteran faculty and benefit from their informal mentoring. Faculty who have college-aged children may also be potential allies, having found that their perspective on the student experience changes when it becomes personal. Seek administrators who have demonstrated a commitment to students, as well as flexibility and adaptability to change. The director or dean may not always be the best person to have on the task force. Planners should seek out administrators who know the institution well, who have the ability to influence policy, and who are receptive to new paradigms.

4. Involve students in the discussion and the delivery systems you design from the very beginning. Too frequently we discuss students and their experiences as if they are raw materials or widgets. They are the best experts on the student experience *as it is*, not just as we believe it to be. Levine (1994) and others have reported that students are the best teachers of other students, and they must be active participants in

> On many other campuses, junior faculty are eager to participate in learning communities because they have an opportunity to collaborate with veteran faculty and benefit from their informal mentoring.

67

their own learning and development. Identify students who are good representatives and spokespersons, who can articulate concerns concisely to both students and administrators. Don't forget that these students are not always the elected leaders, but can be students who stand out as natural leaders among peers.

5. Start with the end in mind. Identify the outcomes you are seeking, and how you will know when you are achieving them. When designing learning communities, design a flowchart with the systems and processes of current programs and services that will be essential to your efforts. Question the necessity of each step in the process, and identify ways in which resources can be linked to each step. Can these be linked with other in-class, out-of-class, or residential experiences? Who are potential partners or stakeholders in each step or in the whole process?

6. Be prepared to compromise. Sacred cows make the best hamburgers. Question which processes are truly essential versus which processes have become victim to the tyranny of custom. Participants need to be able to take risks and have faith that the whole will be greater than the sum of its current parts.

7. Develop an assessment strategy early, and utilize data in the planning and refinement process. Utilize relevant data to help recruit new partners, tailoring your presentation to issues and information in which they will be interested. Academic departments may be unaware that there are "clusters" of students in residence halls which may lend themselves to the formation of a residential learning community. Similarly, the departments may also be unaware of the retention or achievement patterns of their students. Finally, be sure to use a variety of assessment techniques, such as surveys, unobtrusive data (e.g., grade point average, retention, usage rates), focus groups, standardized measures, and personal interviews.

8. Establish and maintain clear levels of communication at all administrative levels. It is not enough that directors are sharing information and ideas. Mid-level and support staff in each area must also be involved in regular communications with each other. Utilize various methods of communication (e-mail, voice mail, meeting minutes, etc.) to keep a broad level of current awareness. Encourage others to share input. Frequently, front line or support staff have important insights into where students experience gaps in academic support services (i.e., where the seams limit effectiveness and success). Be sure to develop a communication strategy to both internal and external constituents, especially on new initiatives that might be misunderstood or encounter resistance.

Conclusion

Students are often unable to integrate new material learned within and without the classroom to achieve a comprehensive learning experience in college. This occurs primarily because campuses are comprised of three distinct zones—the faculty zone, the administrative zone, and the student zone. In a traditional institution, only the student is required to migrate daily between the three zones and attempt to navigate the collegiate experience successfully, hopefully learning something along the way.

This chapter has demonstrated the benefits that can accrue to a campus when well-intentioned people agree on some shared risks; in essence, when we as professionals, accustomed to our own zone agree to enter and travel in another zone. By doing this, we can design integrated learning experiences that transcend the three distinct zones. And, in the process, we can become role models of the behavior that we expect and require of our students. What better way to make administration a form of teaching and learning. The advantages of participation culminate in faculty, administrators, and students all doing the same thing—teaching, learning, and developing.

References

Astin, A. W. (1985). *Achieving academic excellence*. San Francisco: Jossey-Bass.

Blake, E. S. (1979). Classroom and context: An educational dialectic. *Academe, 65,* 280-292.

Blake, E. S. (1996). The yin and yang of student learning in college. *About Campus, 1*(4), 4-9.

Bloland, P. A., Stamatakos, L. C., & Rogers, R. R. (1996). Redirecting the role of student affairs to focus on student learning. *Journal of College Student Development, 37*(2), 217-226.

Gabelnick, F., MacGregor, L., Matthews, R. S., & Smith, B. L. (1990). Learning communities: Creating connections among students, faculty, and disciplines. *New Directions for Teaching and Learning, 41.* San Francisco: Jossey-Bass.

Garland, P. H. (1985). Serving more than students: A critical need for college student personnel services. *ASHE-ERIC Higher Education Report, 7.* Washington, DC: Association for the Study of Higher Education.

Kellogg Commission on the Future of State and Land-Grant Universities. (1997). *Returning to our roots: The student experience.* Washington, DC: National Association of State Universities and Land-Grant Colleges.

Kuh, G. D., Douglas, K. D., Lund, J. P., & Ramin-Gyurnek, J. (1994). Student learning outside the classroom: Transcending artificial boundaries. *ASHE-ERIC Higher Education Report, 8.* Washington, DC: The George Washington University.

Kuh, G. D. (1997, June). *Working together to enhance student learning inside and outside the classroom.* Paper presented at the Annual American Association for Higher Education (AAHE) Assessment and Quality Conference, Miami, FL.

Levine, A. (1994). Guerilla education in residential life. In C. Schroeder, & P. Mable (Eds.), *Realizing the educational potential of residence halls.* San Francisco: Jossey-Bass.

Pascarella, E. T., & Terenzini, P. T. (1991). *How college affects students.* San Francisco: Jossey-Bass.

Pike, G. R. (1996, Fall). A student success story: Freshman interest groups at the University of Missouri-Columbia. *Student Life Studies Abstracts, 1.* (Available from the University of Missouri-Columbia).

Pike, G. R., Schroeder, C. C., & Berry, T. R. (1997). Enhancing the educational impact of residence halls: The relationship between residential learning communities and first-year college experiences and persistence. *Journal of College Student Development, 38*(6), 609-621.

Schroeder, C. C., & Hurst, J. C. (1996). Designing learning environments that integrate curricular and co-curricular experiences. *Journal of College Student Development, 37*(2), 174-181.

Schroeder, C. C., Nicholls, G. E., & Kuh, G. D. (1983). Exploring the rain forest: Testing assumptions and taking risks. In G. D. Kuh (Ed.), Understanding student affairs organizations. *New Directions for Student Services, 23.* San Francisco: Jossey-Bass.

Seymour, D. (1995). *Once upon a campus: Lessons for improving quality and productivity in higher education.* Phoenix: American Council on Education.

Terenzini, P. T., & Pascarella, E. T. (1994). Living with myths: Undergraduate education in America. *Change, 26*(1), 28-32.

Whitt, E. J. (1996). Some propositions worth debating. *About Campus, 1*(4), 31-32.

Wingspread Group on Higher Education. (1993). *An American imperative: Higher expectations for higher education.* Racine, WI: Johnson Foundation.

CHAPTER EIGHT

Learning Communities, Academic Advising, and Other Support Programs

Jack W. Bennett

Before the advent of learning communities and other structures that span the curricular and co-curricular, the work of socializing and supporting students was delegated away from the faculty and toward programs administered by student affairs professionals. As a result, especially in large, public universities, students' academic and social lives were fractured. Freshmen experienced the division most keenly. They went to class—frequently large lectures—and occasionally, in structured laboratories and discussion groups, explored issues and ideas evolving from the lectures. Then students scattered to their jobs, their residence halls, and other homes; real life commenced. As Astin (1993) and others have shown, students' most influential interactions are with their peers, interactions that tend not to overlap with students' intellectual lives. Students move between twin worlds of classes and social life, and the twain rarely meet.

Academic advising and orientation programs have attempted to assimilate students into the university community both academically and socially. However, the press of new student advising frequently reduces the interaction between incoming students and their advisors—be they professional advisors or instructional faculty members—to a focused attempt at building a first-semester schedule. Frequently the advisor-student connection is severed after the initial meeting. Successful orientation programs provide introductions to many aspects of campus life but usually fade away as classes begin. As the excitement of arrival gives way to the regimen of classes and quizzes, the gulf between intellectual and social life becomes so pervasive it seems almost natural. Students adapt; their life at the university flows in parallel channels.

Learning communities attempt to repair the division students experience between their in-class and out-of-class experiences. Academic advising and other student support services necessarily play key roles in the implementation, and, not infrequently, in the design of such programs. Learning communities also provide an educational structure that connects the efforts of student affairs professionals and teaching faculty. This connection begins with the academic advising of incoming students and often persists through shared responsibility for learning communities.

No matter where the impetus for learning communities originates, their consolidation and future growth depends on the sharing of a common vision by all branches of a university community. Therefore, incremental growth of a program, with time to evaluate and adjust, works best. When importing program designs from other colleges and universities, local conditions will dictate adaptations to suit the campus culture. Whether as managers or as consultants, advisors participate in six necessary functions in implementing and managing learning community programs. The six functions are:

1. Deciding how communities will be structured, specifically curricular decisions

2. Assisting students with selecting learning communities and with registration

3. Selecting, supporting, and assessing student peer leaders

4. Administering, or helping to administer, the program

5. Teaching the one-credit seminar/student success component

6. Identifying additional support needs of students and faculty in learning communities

For an extended explanation of the roles academic advisors play, consider the University of Oregon's Freshman Interest Group (FIG) program. The FIG program, conceived in 1982 by the Office of Academic Advising and Student Services, has grown and developed through 16 years of administration by the advising office. Many other programs, based on Oregon's model, acknowledge advising's central role but manage their programs from a different campus office. Whether academic advisors oversee programs or assist and consult with others, they are uniquely qualified to contribute to informed decisions about implementing and managing learning communities.

How Will Learning Communities Be Structured?

Although input from faculty, deans, and department heads is recommended and useful, academic advisors are uniquely well-prepared for this task. Liberated from the narrow view imposed by adherence to a specific academic discipline, advisors perceive how information and pedagogical methods employed in one class can usefully connect with another. For instance, a prelaw FIG at Oregon links a section of Introduction to Native American Literature with United States history, English composition, and a one-credit seminar, "The College Experience." To complete their schedules, most students choose an additional class, probably a foreign language or math class. An experienced advisor, who knew about the history professor's focus on Native American issues, suggested the link. Typically, the history or literature professor would also teach the College Experience course: In this case, it is taught by the prelaw advisor. Experienced advisors learn from their students a superficial knowledge about a great variety of classes. They can apply this knowledge usefully when structuring learning communities.

Selection of and Registration for Learning Communities

This is the traditional role of advisors: Know the curriculum; assess the student; and make connections. When Oregon freshmen receive a brochure detailing the 45 available FIGs, they rank order their first five preferences and mail back the brochure. The brochure also contains descriptions of classes, and students choose their FIG based on the unifying theme as well as the particular linked classes. Frequent telephone and e-mail conversations regarding FIG selection between the advisor and student occur over the summer; when students arrive on campus, they confirm with advisors whether their chosen and assigned FIG is appropriate. Students who do not respond to the mailed invitation to join a FIG may, on a space-available basis and in consultation with an advisor, add a FIG at this time.

The university's registrar developed software that allows students in FIGs to be registered with a keystroke; students are placed in classes upon receipt of their reservation cards. During their initial advising sessions, changes can be negotiated.

Fortunately, by training and temperament, registrars are problem-solvers. Their work as managers of student records and university schedules is technical and complex. Changes in registration procedures for selected students are always potentially contentious. Therefore, the registrar, along with advisors, should be consulted very early in the process of establishing learning communities. Experience suggests that registration in learning communities is inevitably labor-intensive, but problems will be minimized if communication with the registrar is early and ongoing.

Selecting, Supporting, and Assessing Student Leaders

Peer mentoring and leadership are key components of many learning communities programs and are prominent in the University of Oregon FIG model. Each FIG of approximately 25 freshmen has a weekly meeting coordinated by its senior, junior, or sometimes sophomore student leader. Typically, these leaders join a FIG in their freshman year, and subsequently apply to become FIG peer leaders as upperclassmen. Peer leader applicants are screened through written applications and interviews conducted by academic advisors in conjunction with the FIG student staff. Peer leaders are provided a small stipend that is prorated so that repeating leaders receive more than first-time leaders. At Oregon, the number of applicants to become FIG leaders has consistently exceeded the number of positions, which reinforces the prestige of the position.

Peer leaders are involved in the planning of the curricular and co-curricular aspects of their FIG. During a required two-credit FIG leadership course the preceding spring term, leaders develop an agenda for their FIG. Activities can be both academic and social. For instance, the prelaw FIG leaders might arrange a tour of the law school or invite an attorney to talk with the group. The "Understanding Images" FIG might visit a TV studio or attend the theater together. The primary responsibilities of FIG leaders are to build a sense of community in their groups, to acquaint students with campus resources like the library, tutoring centers, and access to computers, and to model attitudes and behaviors conducive to student success. Although academic advising is an important component of the training class, leaders are urged to refer students to professional and faculty advisors for questions beyond their scope.

> The primary responsibilities of FIG leaders are to build a sense of community in their groups, to acquaint students with campus resources like the library, tutoring centers, and access to computers, and to model attitudes and behaviors conducive to student success.

Assisting with Program Administration

Consistent with the philosophy of learning communities—that education is a communal and cooperative enterprise—programs are most likely to thrive when their contributions to improving students' academic and social adjustment are apparent to everyone. Incremental growth allows time for a program to prove itself and garner support. Seldom in a position to coerce anyone on campus, advisors manage effectively only when faculty and administrative officers embrace and support the concept. Learning communities gather momentum, not through directives from a central authority, but from a shared sense that students are being better educated and served. Compared with other programs or departments on campus, academic advising and academic support services are often underfunded considering the programs and services that they provide. The low funding level for this area represents a significant drawback to housing learning communities under the umbrella of academic advising. Therefore, a provost's or dean's support is essential.

When programs are not managed from an advising office, it is axiomatic that advisors and registration staff be included in committees or any other organizing structure. In their book, *Learning Communities: Creating Connections Among Students, Faculty, and Disciplines* (1990), Gabelnick, MacGregor, Matthews, and Smith emphasize this point:

Educating and involving advisors and registration staff in the process of developing learning communities is critical. The staff should be invited to program meetings and seminars as well as planning meetings to get a feel for the programs. Otherwise, misunderstandings can develop. One institution learned that students who had enrolled in a learning community were later persuaded by their advisor to drop out because he did not agree with the concept. At another institution, the Advising Office mistakenly assumed that the learning community was only for honors students and turned away other prospects. A survey of twelve colleges in Washington indicated that more than half of the students were advised into learning communities by the advising and registration offices. Some schools have planning retreats that involve faculty, key administrators and advising and registration staff. This helps avoid miscommunication and broadens ownership in the effort. (p. 46)

Teaching the Student Success Component

Following the highly successful example of freshman seminars at the University of South Carolina, Oregon's FIG program has incorporated a one-credit "College Experience" class. Taught initially only by academic advisors, the class is now more typically taught by professors who also teach a lecture course in the FIG. Teachers prepare for this class by attending workshops at an off-campus location. There are four required elements in the class: (a) academic planning, (b) study skills and time management, (c) campus resources like the library, computing resources, and career center, and (d) a consideration of civil behavior, especially around the issues of alcohol, drugs, and sexuality. The academic planning assignment requires each student to construct a four-year academic plan to fulfill requirements for a degree. Students undecided on a major must posit one to complete this academic planning exercise.

When faculty members teach the course, they frequently recruit help from the advising office in developing the academic planning unit for the course. Advisors contribute through their

comprehensive understanding of general education requirements and their knowledge of educational options, such as the ways in which various majors, minors, and other programs intersect with general requirements. Faculty frequently turn to the professional advising staff to develop a four-year academic planning exercise.

Identifying the Needs of Students in Learning Communities

Students choose particular learning communities, be they FIGs, linked courses, federated learning communities, or something else, because they want to explore ideas that permeate the learning community. When the unifying theme is a professional objective, like medicine, law, engineering, or education, then professional advisors with the relevant expertise should be involved. Career services professionals can also make important contributions to the knowledge base and self-confidence of students.

Advisors know which courses are historically difficult for first-year students and regularly interact with students who are experiencing academic difficulties. When these courses are included in learning communities, advisors can recommend additional ways of supporting student success. Temple University has linked Supplemental Instruction to several of its learning communities. Supplemental Instruction targets historically difficult courses (Martin & Arendale, 1993); students have the option of attending weekly group learning sessions facilitated by an undergraduate who has completed the targeted course successfully with the same instructor in a previous semester. Supplemental Instruction is a natural companion to learning communities because it builds on the value of peers-learning-from-peers that is central to the learning communities model. Conversations with advisors contribute to decisions as to which communities would include Supplemental Instruction.

Making connections is the goal for learning communities, and these six functions for academic advisors demonstrate their central role in making and maintaining connections among students, faculty, and staff. To reasonable people, well-acquainted with traditional methods of delivering education to undergraduates, the advantages of learning communities are obvious. However, any manipulation of the curriculum is politically and technically sensitive. Time spent in face-to-face communication, answering questions, listening carefully, and incorporating useful suggestions is time very well spent. Academic advisors are uniquely qualified to make important contributions to this conversation.

References

Astin, A. W. (1993). *What matters in college? Four critical years revisited*. San Francisco: Jossey-Bass.

Gabelnick, F., MacGregor, J., Matthews, R. S., & Smith, B. L. (Eds.). (1990). Learning communities: Creating connections among students, faculty, and disciplines. *New Directions for Teaching and Learning, 41*. San Francisco: Jossey-Bass.

Martin, D. C., & Arendale, D. R. (1993). *Supplemental Instruction: Improving student success in high-risk courses* (2nd ed.) (Monograph No. 7). Columbia, SC: University of South Carolina, National Resource Center for The Freshman Year Experience.

Chapter Nine

A Natural Linkage—The First-Year Seminar and the Learning Community

Betsy O. Barefoot, Dorothy S. Fidler,
John N. Gardner, Philip S. Moore,
and Melissa R. Roberts

As is evident throughout this monograph, the term "learning community" has been used to describe a variety of structures for linking students and faculty across the curriculum and often the co-curriculum. The chapter authors have also argued for the special value of learning communities in the first college year as a means to accomplish, simultaneously, both academic and social integration of new students (Tinto, 1993).

Another curricular innovation designed to connect students more intentionally to the academic and social spheres of campus life is the first-year seminar. First-year (a.k.a., freshman, new student) seminars, offered since the 1880s, have, in the 1990s, become nearly ubiquitous in American higher education. Research conducted in 1997 by the National Resource Center for The First-Year Experience indicates that over 70% of American colleges and universities offer such a course.

Because learning communities and first-year seminars share many common objectives, it seems only natural to link these two concepts, and such a linkage has taken place on a number of campuses. According to findings of the 1997 National Survey of First-Year Seminars, approximately 14% of institutions with a first-year seminar link it to other courses in the curriculum. The purpose of this chapter is to provide a rationale for such a union, but also to describe some of these special learning communities in depth and the research that demonstrates their effectiveness in improving student retention, grade point averages, and overall satisfaction with college.

The Role of a First-Year Seminar in a Learning Community

Learning communities exist along a continuum. On one end are structural linkages only—linked courses in which there is little or no attention paid to linking instruction or intentionally creating a sense of community among the participating students. On the opposite end are those exemplary learning communities in which faculty collaboration, cross-disciplinary instruction, and a strong sense of academic and social camaraderie exist for students. While exemplary models occur at all locations along the continuum, the more integrated models of learning communities often offer students a richer set of experiences than mere structural linkages. First-year seminars can play a unique and meaningful role in moving a learning community along the continuum to a higher level of integration in the following ways:

- The first-year seminar can be the linchpin, the glue that lends coherency and unity to the learning community. The seminar can transcend the individual courses and move students (and faculty) to the next level of interdisciplinary, interconnected thinking and writing.

- The seminar can be the most active learning context within the learning community, lending itself easily to application of concepts, critical thinking, and classroom activities.

- Student affairs professionals often have a planning or co-teaching role in first-year seminars. The learning community potentially extends that role to other courses so that closer ties exist between the curriculum and co-curriculum.

- The seminar can be the vehicle for teaching students many learning strategies necessary for success in the discipline-based courses such as computer, study, and library skills.

- The seminar may be the component of the learning community that utilizes peer instruction most effectively.

- The seminar allows student-to-student relationships to develop and transfer to other courses in the learning community. These friendships promote the creation of study groups and general support, both academic and social.

- The seminar can be the site for first-year academic advising and for assessment of student characteristics and learning during the first college year.

Research evidence suggests that, with or without a first-year seminar, learning communities yield improved student performance; but the seminar has the potential to move the learning community to a higher level of effectiveness for students, faculty, and the institution.

Exemplary Integrated Models

The following six institutions link first-year seminars into learning communities on their campuses, although their ways of accomplishing this linkage vary.

Indiana University-Purdue University Indianapolis (IUPUI)

At this open-admissions institution, learning communities were developed to meet the academic and social needs of a diverse student population that includes first-generation college students, students with full-time jobs, and students with families. After taking placement tests, 80% of the first-year class is required to take developmental courses in reading, writing, and/or mathematics. However, there are no full-time tenure track faculty members teaching developmental courses; hence, in the past there was little to no interaction between faculty and many first-year students. The learning community program, developed in 1994, has provided a solution to this problem.

IUPUI's learning community program was largely developed by faculty members. Since its beginnings the program has grown, and the University plans to offer 73 learning communities in fall of 1998. These learning communities will consist of the first-year seminar, modeled on the University of South Carolina's University 101 and a disciplinary course. A faculty member along with a librarian, an academic advisor, a student mentor, and a technology specialist teach the seminar collaboratively. The faculty "team anchor" also teaches the linked disciplinary course. This increases contact between faculty and first-year students. Primary goals of the learning community include establishing connections to the university community, increasing student involvement, and improving collaboration among faculty and students.

The learning community program functions as part of a larger academic support unit to promote greater retention, higher grade point averages, and other positive outcomes. On-campus research shows that the program has a significant impact on persistence to the spring semester. Additionally, when African-American males, the sub-population with the lowest retention rates, participate in the learning community program, they have significantly higher persistence rates when compared to nonparticipating African-American males and all other undergraduates (Borden & Rooney, 1998). Learning communities at IUPUI are discussed further in Chapter 6 of this monograph.

Contact:
Scott Evenbeck
Dean, University College
815 West Michigan Street
Indianapolis, IN 46202
(317)274-5032
e-mail: evenbeck@iupui.edu

Lyndon State College

A unique learning community approach exists at Lyndon State College in Vermont. The institution groups students into pods of between three and eight members. Each small pod enrolls in two to four courses in common the first semester. The courses also enroll students who are not members of the learning pods. Students in a pod share the new student seminar and a first-year writing course, a first-year math course, or another general education course.

The program began in the summer of 1997 with approximately 375 student participants. Administrators and faculty formed the pods using placement test results as well as information provided by the students concerning course preferences. Plans are underway to alter the pod model for the

> . . . when African-American males . . . participate in the learning community program, they have significantly higher persistence rates when compared to nonparticipating African-American males and all other undergraduates (Borden & Rooney, 1998).

academic year 1998-1999 to make the system more efficient. For example, the institution plans to coordinate course offerings to provide more pods next year. In addition, Lyndon State plans to coordinate two other learning community programs for Summer 1998 and the academic year 1998-1999. One approach will pair either a writing or math course with a discipline-based course. The institution plans to offer at least four of these pairs of courses in the fall of 1998. The College also plans to offer a program to 20 at-risk new students who volunteer to participate. These students will compose a cohort that will share writing, math, psychology, new-student seminar, and another general education course. They will also have the opportunity to meet regularly with faculty advisors and student support staff.

Lyndon State has not conducted any formal research on the Learning Community program. However, preliminary informal examination of the program suggests that this approach may have improved the retention rate of new students from the Fall 1997 to the Spring 1998 semester.

Contact:
Sheryl Hruska
Associate Academic Dean
College Road
Lyndonville, VT 05851
(802)626-6497
e-mail: hruskas@king.lsc.vsc.edu.

Northern Michigan University

First-Year Experience Blocks constitute the learning communities at Northern Michigan University. These FYE Blocks include the University's Freshman Seminar. The university offered 18 blocks in the fall of 1998. Twelve were designed for students with a specific major or discipline. Six were available to all majors or to students who have not declared a major. FYE Blocks offer a minimum of three courses including traditional liberal studies or general education courses that may be laboratory sections, discussion sessions, or lecture classes. One block that is open to undeclared majors provides a residential option for students to live in the same residence hall. Most of the major-specific blocks designate departmental faculty as freshman seminar instructors.

Northern Michigan University began using the FYE Block system in the fall of 1995 and has tracked the success rate of students who participated in blocks since that time. Research results show increases in student retention for FYE Block participants. When compared with other students, a greater percentage of FYE Block participants have higher GPAs, and a significantly higher number of participants are on clear academic status (2.0 GPA or better). Gains in each area measured are evident every year.

Contact:
Laura Soldner
Director of the First-Year Experience Program
140 Presque Isle Avenue
Marquette, MI 49855
(906)227-2672
e-mail: lsoldner@nmu.edu

San Diego State University

San Diego State University's learning community program has been in place 13 years. The program began as an Intensive Learning Experience Program in 1985 and provided opportunities for under-represented students. In 1992, the program evolved into the Integrated Curriculum Program and now comprises a major part of the University's Learning Center Program as well as a major part of the Freshman Success Program curriculum.

Any student may register to participate in an Integrated Curriculum Package. An Integrated Curriculum Package offers a cluster of courses that are scheduled in a block. Students in a particular block will usually take five courses together in a small group of 12-25 students. Each Integrated Curriculum Package contains a general education or major requirement, a one-unit study group, a required writing, math, or chemistry course, University Seminar, and additional classes chosen by the individual. In fall of 1997,

70 Integrated Curriculum Packages were offered at the university.

San Diego State University's research findings reveal that students who participate in an Integrated Curriculum Package are more successful than the rest of the freshman class. For the fall semester of 1996, the University found that a lower percentage of Integrated Curriculum participants were put on academic probation. Additionally, the Integrated Curriculum participants had higher retention rates than the rest of the freshman class.

Contact:
Ronald Young
Director of Thomas B. Day Freshman Success Programs
5500 Campanile Drive
San Diego, CA 92182
(619)594-0419
e-mail: ryoung@mail.sdsu.edu.

Temple University

The Fox School of Business and Management at Temple University links a two-credit freshman seminar to other courses in its learning communities. This school requires all entering freshmen to enroll in four linked courses: a law lecture, a writing course, a computer science course (including lecture, recitation, and lab), and the freshman seminar.

A recent qualitative study at Temple examined, among other things, the varying uses of the freshman seminar in the different learning communities on campus. By using freshman seminars as part of the learning community, the School of Business and Management hopes to improve retention by coordinating the efforts of the instructors of the linked courses with the students' academic advisors. Other goals of the freshman seminars are to provide professional development opportunities for students and foster a better understanding of the Business School. The study found advantages to the freshman seminar/learning community linkage. The students in each cohort experience a greater sense of camaraderie due to the amount of time they spend together. Also, the research suggests that the learning community may facilitate a strong relationship between students and their advisor.

The School of Communications and Theater and the College of Arts and Sciences also use the learning community approach, but until recently, the freshman seminar, "Learning for the New Century," has not been linked to other courses. In the fall of 1998, nine learning communities that intentionally link the freshman seminar were established in the College of Arts and Sciences. Like most courses of its kind, the freshman seminar at Temple addresses issues of college life and discusses study strategies appropriate to discipline-based courses in the learning community.

Seminars are also offered for students in other undergraduate schools and colleges. The School of Communications and Theater offers a stand-alone version for its freshmen; and in 1995, the Learning Communities Program developed a freshman seminar for students in liberal arts. Initially the seminar was not linked to a specific learning community, but entering freshmen were encouraged to register for both a seminar and a learning community. In the fall of 1998, however, nine learning communities intentionally linked the seminar with two discipline-based courses. Like most courses of its kind, the freshman seminar at Temple addresses issues of college life and discusses learning strategies appropriate to the discipline-based courses in the learning community. In 1999, more than half of the learning communities will feature two linked courses and a section of the seminar.

Contact:
Jodi Levine
Director of First-Year Programs
Philadelphia, PA 19122
(215)204-1937
e-mail: jodih@vm.temple.edu.

University of Missouri-Columbia

The University of Missouri at Columbia offers Freshman Interest Groups (FIGs) which are theme-related learning communities. Each FIG enrolls between 10 and 15 students. Commonly, the students in a particular FIG live on the same floor in the same residence hall with an upper-division peer advisor. The peer advisor typically has a major related to the FIG theme and co-facilitates the one-hour freshman seminar component of the cluster of courses with a faculty or staff member ("A Student Success Story: Freshman Interest Groups at the University of Missouri-Columbia," 1996).

A 1996 study examined the effects of the FIG program on student learning, achievement, and retention. When compared with non-enrolled students, FIG students had a higher rate of retention and significantly higher GPAs for the fall of 1995 ("A Student Success Story: Freshman Interest Groups at the University of Missouri-Columbia," 1996).

Researchers administered the *MU Freshman Survey* and found that FIG participants had significantly higher levels of academic integration and institutional commitment. The survey also revealed that the FIG participants made greater advances in communication skills and general education than other students. Students also responded to the *College Student Experiences Questionnaire* and reported information about first-year involvement. FIG participants reported greater informal interaction with faculty outside class and higher rates of interaction with peers. In addition, the content of these interactions was likely to be intellectual in nature ("A Student Success Story: Freshman Interest Groups at the University of Missouri-Columbia," 1996). Learning communities at the University of Missouri-Columbia are discussed in detail in Chapter 7.

Frankie Minor
Director of Residence Life
125 Jesse Hall
Columbia, MO 65211
(573)882-7275
e-mail: reslffm@showme.missouri.edu.

Other Research Findings on Integrated First-Year Seminar/Learning Community Models

Although much has been written about both learning communities and first-year seminars, research evidence to date on the impact of the inclusion of the integrated seminar in the learning community is limited at best. A search of the literature, including both print and electronic media, found brief descriptions of another ten such programs that have been the subject of on-campus research. These brief descriptions, grouped by institutional size, follow.

Institutions with 20,000 or More Students

Illinois State University. "Connections" was established to enhance student recruitment, to facilitate the transition of new freshmen to campus life, and to improve first-year academic performance and retention. Students take two or three subject-related courses together, along with a one-hour, non-credit first-year seminar. The seminar, described as an extended first-year orientation course, meets once a week to pursue academic and social endeavors in an informal setting. The program has been well received by faculty and students, and has been shown to have a positive impact on persistence (A. E. Dillingham, personal communication, April 27, 1998; Dillingham, Harris, & Kalianov, 1996).

Of the 4,200 freshmen, approximately 2,000 participate in the program. Over the next three years, the percent of the first-year class participating in the program is predicted to increase to about 70%. . .

Northern Illinois University. The theme of the linked courses program is "Education in the Year 2000." The goal of the program is to attract students of color into teacher education and to increase their persistence. During the first semester, a first-year experience course, a basic writing course, and a college reading course are linked. The second semester links college reading and study strategies, general writing, and introductory educational foundations courses. The first-year experience course is called "Counseling Help and Assistance Necessary for a College Education," or CHANCE. In this course, students meet weekly with a counselor from Educational Services and Programs, and occasionally meet with an advisor from the College of Education. The seminar acclimates students to the university environment and assists students in developing a working knowledge of resources that promote persistence. The seminar also familiarizes students with university requirements that affect future teachers (*CHANCE*, 1998; Costello & Stahl, 1996).

The Pennsylvania State University. Linked courses are available only in the College of Liberal Arts. The purpose of the linked courses program is to provide first-semester students with the opportunity to interact with top faculty who are active researchers. Two or three general education courses are linked with a first-year seminar limited to 20 students per class. The three-credit orientation to college seminar helps students think about their educational goals, apply what they learn, and reflect upon why they chose to attend Penn State. All of this should assist in socializing students to university life. Faculty are given $500 for course enhancement. The focus of the seminar is learning for the students as well as for the faculty. While no formal assessment results are available, anecdotal evidence indicates that faculty embrace the opportunity to learn about things they have always wanted to study. After teaching the seminar, faculty exhibit positive outcomes such as excitement and the development of a community of learning with other faculty and students. In addition, students get to discover early if they wish to continue in their chosen major. This allows them to change majors without failure or loss of credits (*Freshman Seminar Symposium*, 1998).

University of Washington. The primary purpose of the linked courses program is to introduce students to college life and to help students overcome the problems of attending a large institution by getting them involved during the first semester. First-year students may enroll in a cluster of courses, Freshman Interest Groups (FIGs), which are focused around a theme such as business, liberal arts, science, or engineering. In the fall quarter of 1997, over 70 FIGs were offered. Each FIG enrolled approximately 22 students in each cluster of courses. Over one third of the Fall 1997 first-year class participated in the program. Although results from a major program evaluation are not yet available, its success can be measured by its popularity: Of the 4,200 first-year students, approximately 2,000 participate in the program. Over the next three years, the percent of the first-year class participating in the program is predicted to increase to about 70% (*Freshman Interest Group Program*, 1998; J. Johnson, personal communication, April 29, 1998; "Learning Community Programs in Washington,"1996; "New Student Programs," 1997). A more detailed description of learning communities at the University of Washington is provided in Chapter 4.

Washington State University. The linked courses program is designed to introduce new students to learning at the college level by promoting discussion about learning within and across academic disciplines. A two-credit, first-year seminar is linked with one or two introductory courses in such diverse areas as engineering, animal sciences, psychology, and English. Topics addressed in the first-year seminar include accessing academic resources, expectations of academic culture, analysis and synthesis of linked course information, as well as information from non-linked courses, problem solving, and epistemology. The program takes advantage of interactive technology, such as computer-based instruction and asynchronous dialog among peers, facilitators, and instructors. The classes are limited to 15 students, with as many as 30 sections being offered during the fall semesters. While assessment information regarding the success of this program is unavailable, the program lists the following as potential advantages of this first-year program: improved academic performance, better persistence, increased faculty contact, improved cognitive development, and a more realistic self-appraisal of academic ability (*WSU Creates New Freshman Seminar Program*, 1996; *WSU Freshman Seminars: Information*, 1997).

Institutions with Fewer than 20,000 Students:

Everett Community College. "Women on the Move Toward a Four-Year Degree," in existence for 10 years, assists females in completing their two-year degree and matriculating to a four-year institution. A core math, psychology, or sociology course is paired with an English composition class. Topics for the compositions in the English course relate to the other linked course. In addition, a two-credit orientation to college course is included in the cluster to give the students an opportunity to discuss how the subjects are related. Students participating in the program had higher grades and better completion rates at the two-year and four-year levels. Unfortunately, the program has recently been suspended due primarily to a lack of institutional support. The program is being re-engineered as an evening program for women who work (J. Dunn, personal communication, April 28, 1998; *Learning Communities Directory*, 1998b; *What's Happening: Learning Community and Faculty Exchanges at Participating Institutions*, 1991).

Frostburg State University. This linked courses program assists new students in developing academic and peer relationships. Two or three courses related in theme are linked with a one-credit, first-year orientation seminar taught by the students' advisor. There are currently 10 clusters available, and class size is limited to 25 students. Students participating in the program get better grades during the first semester, form stronger ties with students and faculty, and achieve greater levels of personal development (*All About Learning Communities*, 1998; T. Bowling, personal communication, April 27, 1998).

Northern Kentucky University. This pilot learning communities program is designed to improve the recruitment and retention of first-year students, enhance learning, provide an integrated social and academic environment for both students and faculty, and build a sense of community and attachment to the institution. A course cluster includes a base class, which has an enrollment of 23-27 students, and two other introductory classes in disciplines such as sociology, psychology, biology, history, and geology. The base course is either a first-year orientation seminar, English composition, or speech. The first-year orientation seminar provides a better opportunity to integrate the content of the linked courses. Instructors in a cluster are not required to collaborate, but are encouraged to do so. In addition, faculty development opportunities are planned, such as guest lecturers, brown bag lunch meetings, and workshops. While no assessment information is available for this pilot program, there are plans for performing quantitative evaluation of retention and grades; faculty and students interviews and surveys are also planned (*Learning Communities Pilot*, 1996).

Texas A&M University at Corpus Christi. The linked courses program was initially used to assist the institution in switching from an upper-division to a four-year comprehensive university. A first-year, writing-across-the-curriculum course is the base course for the cluster, which also includes two introductory courses and a first-year seminar. The first-year seminar strives to assist students in academic and social transitions to college life, and to increase personal development. A learning log is kept by students in the first-year seminar to interconnect learning from the other three courses in the cluster (Durrwachter, Jackson, & Spencer, 1996; *University Core Curriculum Program*, 1998).

University of Northern Colorado. The Academic Advantage Program is geared toward new students who may need developmental assistance, or who may merely wish more assistance with advising. The program is in response to student requests for better advisement, a more cohesive academic experience, and assistance in adapting to college life. The English composition class is linked with either a sociology, psychology, or history course. In addition, a new student orientation seminar is used to strengthen the linkage among the courses. The linked course program has been shown to have a positive impact on first- and second-year persistence and on GPAs. These advantages are experienced by all types of students, including academically at-risk students and students of color ("Fostering Student Connections and Student Success," 1996; *Learning Communities Directory*, 1996).

Summary

The programs described in this chapter have been identified as consisting of introductory courses linked with first-year seminars. The seminars, ranging in level of credit from zero to three cred-

its, unify all the courses in the cluster since the first-year seminar offers the opportunity for integrative discussions. The clusters consist of one to four other courses that may or may not be thematically related. The reported goals of these programs with linked courses are shown below in order of prevalence:

- Increase persistence
- Assist in the transition to college
- Provide a cohesive first-year learning experience
- Increase academic performance
- Improve recruitment
- Increase commitment to the institution
- Increase sense of community
- Increase student/faculty interactions
- Involve students in university life
- Increase personal development

The reported gains made by students in these programs with linked courses are shown below in order of prevalence:

- Increased retention
- Increased academic performance
- Increased student/faculty interactions
- Greater sense of community
- A more cohesive first-year learning experience
- Easier transition to college
- Stronger commitment to the institution
- Increased involvement in college life
- Increased personal development

Conclusion

Including a first-year seminar among the linked courses in a learning community has great potential for creating the bonds across disciplines that faculty and academic deans hope for and seek on their own campuses. These bonds between student and student, between faculty and student, and between faculty in different disciplines can lift the educational experience to a new level of collaboration and cognitive development for all. The first-year seminar may well be the most effective way to facilitate creation of bonds and connections across disciplines, students, and faculty. It is in the first-year seminar that faculty integrate new learning from several discipline-based courses into a coherent whole.

This chapter has highlighted some model learning communities with seminars that, to a varying degree, strive for the highest levels of cognitive and social development for their students; and, as we all know experientially and intuitively (for there is little supportive data), faculty development is an inherent part of such a learning community. Those who teach in truly collaborative learning communities also expand their own cognitive and social development and find that this is an exciting venue for faculty renewal. In sum, the potential of a learning community with a first-year seminar integrated into its curriculum has been realized on a few campuses. The model programs exist; now is the time for more institutions of higher education to incorporate these exemplary programs into their own curriculum.

References

All about learning communities. (1998) [online]. Available HTTP://www.fsu.umd.edu/admin/lc/overview.htm

Borden, V., & Rooney, P. (1998). *Evaluating and assessing learning communities.* Department of Information Management and Research. Indiana University-Purdue University Indianapolis, 1-20.

CHANCE. (1998) [online]. Available HTTP://www.niu.edu/esp/chance/chance.html

Costello, M. S., & Stahl, N. A. (1996, November). *Promoting diversity: A learning community project for college reading programs and teacher education programs.* Paper presented at the meeting of the College Reading Association, Charleston, SC.

Dillingham, A. E., Harris, E., & Kalianov, C. (1996). Initial assessment of a large learning community program. *Proceedings of Second National Conference on Students in Transition: Coming and Going - Transitions Along the Collegiate Journey,* (pp. 39-40). Columbia: National Resource Center for The Freshman Year Experience and Students in Transition.

Durrwachter, P., Jackson, R., & Spencer, M., K. (1996). Enabling the transition to college: using writing in a collaborative freshman experience. *Proceedings of Second National Conference on Students in Transition: Coming and Going - Transitions Along the Collegiate Journey,* (pp. 39-40). Columbia: National Resource Center for The Freshman Year Experience and Students in Transition.

Fostering student connections and student success: The cluster and academic advantage programs at the University of Northern Colorado. (1996). *Washington Center News, 10*(2), 9-10.

Freshman interest group program. (1998) [online]. Available: HTTP://catsis.weber.edu/FYE/default.html

Freshman seminar symposium. (1998) [online]. Available: HTTP://www.psu.edu/celt/freshman.html

Learning communities directory. (1996) [online]. Available HTTP: //192.211.16.13/katlinks/washcntr/learncom/state/colo/list/unc.html

Learning communities directory. (1998) [online]. Available HTTP: //192.211.16.13/katlinks/washcntr/learncom/state/wash/list/evcc.html

Learning communities pilot. (1996) [online]. Available: HTTP://www.nku.edu/~garns/lc_report1.html

Learning community programs in Washington. (1996). *Washington Center News,10*(2), 30.

Longer-term effects of freshman interest groups on students' college experiences and educational outcomes. (1997). *Missouri University Student Life Abstracts, 5.*

The MU freshman interest groups homepage. (1996) [online]. Available: HTTP://www.missouri.edu/~figwww/oldfiles/index.html

New student programs, University of Washington. (1997). *Getting started: A guide to Academic programs for freshmen* [Brochure]. Seattle, WA: Author.

A student success story: Freshman interest groups at the University of Missouri-Columbia (1996). *University Student Life Abstracts,1*, 1-4.

Tinto, V. (1993). *Leaving college: Rethinking the causes and cures of student attrition* (2nd ed.). Chicago: University of Chicago Press.

University core curriculum program. (1998) [online]. Available HTTP: //www.tamucc.edu/uccp

What's happening: Learning community and faculty exchanges at participating institutions. (1991). *Washington Center News, 6*(1), 31.

WSU creates new freshman seminar program (1996). *Washington Center News, 10*(2), 25.

WSU freshman seminars: Information. (1997) [online]. Available HTTP: //salc.wsu.edu/fs/fsinfo.asp

Chapter Ten

Learning Communities in the Community College

Valerie A. Bystrom

A variety of people come to community colleges for all sorts of reasons; for example, at Seattle Central Community College, culinary arts students in tall white hats set out an enviable luncheon buffet in the Atrium. Over lunch tables, animated students converse in American Sign Language; others compare notes about a calculus problem. Some students have gray hair; others have dreadlocks, shaved heads, or finger waves courtesy of students in the cosmetology program. Students are speaking Japanese, Thai, Tagalog, Russian, Chinese, Spanish, Persian, Vietnamese; the jazz ensemble is playing "Take Five"; other students are recruiting volunteers for a lobbying trip to the state capital; a student knocks on my office door and asks to borrow a collection of Alexander Pope's poems.

In addition to such vitality and diversity, obvious benefits of attending a community college include convenience, low tuition, and small classes. Students live off campus, perhaps with their families; they work part-time or full-time jobs to help pay for school; they walk or ride the bus to campus. Tuition for vocational technical programs is significantly less than at four-year institutions. Because classes are small, students in college-transfer classes can receive more personal attention than they would in entry-level classes at a local university. There are drawbacks, however, to teaching and learning at a community college.

Funding for community colleges is generally not lavish; in some states it is tight, and in others barely adequate. Despite budgetary constraints, community colleges strive to offer as many programs as possible to prepare students for employment and for college transfer. Vocational programs need equipment, and they need to keep pace with advancing technologies. When funding is available, the question becomes how to assemble a comprehensive technical program. The budget for apparel design, for instance, or respiratory therapy may allow for one, perhaps two, faculty members. To serve students bound for other institutions of higher education, community colleges offer a wide range of college-transfer courses corresponding to those taught at other two-year and four-year colleges and universities in the vicinity. The struggle to keep pace with the accelerated proliferation of computer-related technologies further strains already tight budgets.

For students, the convenience and economy of community colleges often promote a sense of casualness and anonymity. Since transfer students pass through community colleges like travelers through hub airports, they often do not have the same sense of an alma mater as students at small, private institutions or at universities. A community college, after all, is often seen as the place to fulfill general education requirements before moving on to a four-year college or university. Whether in a vocational or a college-transfer program, if a student must leave school in the middle of a quarter, the social and financial repercussions are probably less than they would be if leaving a four-year institution. No doubt many students withdraw because they have pressing family responsibilities, but a take-it-or-leave-it attitude about education has a negative impact on retention statistics leading to discouraged college administrators.

Alexander Astin (1993) suggests that students persist in college when strong and meaningful interactions exist among students and between students and faculty. Certainly, students who transfer from community colleges to larger state institutions often remark that classes at the community college are more personal. Even so, an extraordinarily diverse student body often faces a dismal repetitiveness in community college courses because teachers and administrators are, or feel, obliged to provide replaceable, reproducible introductory courses that are transferable to several other state institutions.

Traditionally, a student has little choice but to take "Something 110" (or 210) in which they learn basic concepts and vocabulary while surveying a discipline or field of knowledge, but "Something 110" is knowledge oddly abstracted. Teachers of "Something 110" are expected to prepare students for transfer into higher level courses, yet how much information students are expected to know may be vaguely understood. Using standard textbooks in the field becomes a way of ensuring that students have gotten what they need. So teaching "Something 110" can be a numbing experience for faculty who must plod through textbooks for three classes per quarter for many years. At most community colleges, a standard teaching load is comprised of three courses per quarter (or forty-five hours per year).

For young, well-trained faculty members coming from graduate school, this heavy load of basic courses seems the most onerous aspect of teaching in community colleges. Part-time teachers, especially, those who commute from school to school, may feel just as standard and replaceable as the courses. At four-year institutions, freshmen face larger classes, and assistant professors' teaching loads may be heavy, but there are also upper-division courses for which students understand they are preparing. These courses and perhaps graduate courses enrich the college conversation.

At community colleges, administrators and faculty have the opportunity to maximize the advantages of their institutions and to ameliorate some disadvantages by redesigning curriculum as learning communities. Learning communities ease the tensions often associated with highly diverse and transient populations by building collegiality in the community college. For faculty, links, clusters, and coordinated studies provide welcoming and supportive colleagues and offer every opportunity to take the onus off teaching and shift it to learning in introductory courses. Learning communities allow students and teachers to meet and to transcend the demands for regularization and uniformity. In addition, learning communities: (a) can allow vocational teachers new opportunities for ensuring student success and satisfaction in solid, comprehensive programs and (b) can promote even stronger connections between the college and the surrounding community and the surrounding natural environment.

Simply Linking Two Classes

Introducing even a simple learning community—a linked class—can transform a teaching and learning experience. A handy model links a skills course, perhaps English 101, to an introductory-level content course in a discipline.

The logistics are easy and cost-free, requiring only that advisors and the computer understand that students who sign up for the English course also sign up for the content course. A link, however, costs teachers time, as much of it as they are willing to give. Let's say an anthropology teacher and a composition teacher want to link beginning writing and cultural anthropology. They may visit each other's classes; if possible, they may have release time to attend each other's courses. Before the quarter starts, they meet and plan. Fundamental questions come up—what are they teaching and why?

At Yakima Community College, for instance, two instructors wanted to revise biology from a lecture/exam model to one including more group work that could then be linked with a speech class. But they wondered about transferability and about coverage—could it be that they need not cover everything in the textbook? How could they best prepare students for the next required courses? So they simply asked the teachers of physiology and zoology exactly what they expected students to know and then made sure students in the new biology curriculum learned it.

They talk about their work, about their disciplines, and about what students can gain from the connection. They may decide to rearrange all their work around a common theme or a set of questions.

Having decided exactly what must be covered, the two instructors continue to meet and talk. Perhaps the anthropology teacher has felt bruised by English since high school, and the English teacher has doubts about ethnocentric prowling in other people's cultures. They talk about their work, about their disciplines, and about what students can gain from the connection. They may decide to rearrange all their work around a common theme or a set of questions. In addition to, or in place of, textbooks, they order ethnographies, novels, poetry, and essays. As they talk about how they teach, new ideas for group work, workshops, computer searches, field trips, films, guest speakers, performances, and student presentations may come up.

One could argue a teacher does not require a link to do innovative things in the classroom. Yet working with someone helps; two people seem to generate and to construct better workshops than either can alone. At Seattle Central Community College, collaboration with other faculty in learning communities is the surest route to innovation. Further, Finley (1990) reports that before learning communities, many faculty were well into "burn out, " and the "stimulation and support resulting from the team-teaching experience stopped a few from leaving the profession altogether" (p. 52).

Once the hypothetical course is under way, even more possibilities open up. Rather than seeming like a tedious requirement, the critical thinking and writing skills in composition have direct application and benefit as students tackle anthropology issues and assignments. Terms taken for granted when writing an essay on family customs and traditions for the English course may be put into question when used in anthropology class. "Objectivity" may mean one thing in English and another in anthropology. The students' curiosity about topics unforeseen by the faculty and their rich cultural backgrounds can also drive the structure and content of the course. Often astounded that professors sometimes disagree, students realize they must discern, think critically, and make judgments as they notice the complementarity, the overlapping, or the friction between the disciplines. As different ways of thinking come in contact, new ideas may sprout in the interstices. Assumptions in English composition and in anthropology become connected to other realities and are stretched and pierced and deepened.

Just as with this hypothetical example, a simple link between an English course and a content course promotes the collegiality and the significant conversation at the heart of an intellectual community. Students and faculty rediscover the great pleasure of learning from each other. As one faculty member noted, he is now getting an education he missed the first time around. The ongoing conversation about their work and about (and with) their students radically alters the experience of teaching a linked course. Faculty members, who may not otherwise even meet, become friends while students develop closer ties with each other. Faculty and students converse more candidly about ideas and experiences. Surrounded by a deep investment in teaching and learning and supported by collaboration with students and faculty, students develop a different attitude about their educations. The learning communities created in even a simple linked course may make a huge difference in a student's decisions about school.

Customizing a Link

Community college faculty have developed several ways to structure linked courses. At Centralia Community College, for instance, in linked sections of ethics and political science two hours of each week are set aside for faculty members and students to meet together. Students have the responsibility in this seminar to discuss issues that cut across both courses. Taking this responsibility is part of the students' learning, while helping them to take it, part of the teaching. Both teachers join the seminar and try to provide models of civil disagreement that some students will observe for the first time.

Since 1979, students working toward an associate of arts degree at LaGuardia Community College take the first quarter of English composition in a cluster of courses. Along with composition, students take a course in writing a research paper, two other courses from science, social science, or the arts, and an integrating seminar. For instance, the cluster "Freedom and Seeing" includes composition, research paper writing, introduction to philosophy, and introduction to art. "Work, Labor and Business in American Literature" includes the English courses, an introduction to sociology, and a humanities course. A cluster designed spe-

cifically for students entering the business program includes English composition, an introduction to economics, and an introduction to business. Faculty members who participate in the clusters rewrite their syllabi to pursue themes, to sequence presentations, and to give assignments that make teaching and learning in the cluster more coherent. The composition classes also become an integrating seminar for students' discussions and writing about issues they cover in other classes. Further, as the cluster often occurs in a student's first semester of school, a freshman at this large urban institution, has, at the outset, the support of a community of students and faculty.

> Faculty members who participate in the clusters rewrite their syllabi to pursue themes, to sequence presentations, and to give assignments that make teaching and learning in the cluster more coherent.

If certain courses in a program, a vocational program for instance, are obstacles for students, linking them with a skills course can help clear the hurdle. A link between College Study Skills and Biology 101 at Spokane Falls Community College has dramatically increased the number of students successfully completing this first-year science course. Faculty who teach the College Reading and Study Skills course indicate that while students know they should study outside class, they are unsure of how to approach a course like biology. The purpose of the link is to help students develop their own strategies for success. Faculty in the linked program stress that instructors responsible for study skills courses should also attend the linked content course so they will understand the learning strategies best suited to the content. A review of students' learning journals demonstrates students' attitudes are changing. What they first thought was extra busy work, they now realize are keys to learning; students express greater responsibility for their own learning. They not only accept the benefits of working in groups but also begin to demand from each other significant preparation for group work. Because the link with Biology 101 proved so successful, this year the study skills course was also linked to two vocational courses, an introduction to gerontology and a course in the hearing impaired program.

Fully Integrated Links

Most links at Spokane Falls are structured so that a cohort of students takes each of the linked classes. Enough students consistently enroll so that teachers can integrate fully the biology link. Forty to fifty biology students meet for two hours daily; the biology instructor and the study-skills instructor team teach the program. For all of them, the link represents two-thirds of their schedules. The two-hour block offers faculty more flexibility in sequencing assignments and planning in-class activities.

While links between English and either history or social science are easily implemented, the integration may break down between two apparently disparate courses like English and algebra. Faculty at Bellevue Community College have risen to the challenge, creating "The Basic Advantage," a fully integrated link of pre-college algebra and pre-college English. They planned this program with the basic assumption that the best way for a student to demonstrate knowledge of math is to articulate an understanding of the concepts. The topic for all writing assignments is math. In one assignment, students must respond to a terrorist bomb threat at an airport near a school. Given information about the force of the bomb, students write a paper, using charts and graphs for illustration, determining whether it is necessary to evacuate the school.

To make this math/English link successful, faculty must first spend up-front time helping entering students function productively as members of a learning community. Faculty must also help students understand that "the right way" may not exist: There are many correct ways of solving an equation or writing a sentence. Second, the link also requires particular clarity from faculty about the connections to be made between math and English and how to exploit them for the students' advantage. Finally, faculty must integrate the concepts, the contents, the materials, and the assignments as much as possible so that students appreciate that the two disciplines are interdependent, that English and math are not exclusive languages.

For many program activities—such as lectures, presentations, films, and field trips—the students and teachers all meet together. At other times students work in smaller groups. A central piece of coordinated studies at Seattle Central is the book seminar. Students divide into groups of 20 to 25 and along with one teacher meet for two hours twice a week to discuss the book at hand. In the tradition begun by Alexander Meiklejohn (1932) at the University of Wisconsin and passed to us by The Evergreen State College, we build coordinated programs around significant primary texts, not textbooks. For the most part, the books are chosen to develop the theme of the program, but sometimes program themes arise because people want passionately to use certain books. Usually, seminars cover one book a week and the selection of the books is critical because they carry so much of the program content. Using books this way will seem familiar to literature teachers but less so to faculty members who teach in the social sciences and physical sciences. The challenge and the reward are in teaching the fundamentals of an introductory anthropology course, for instance, not with a textbook but with texts like the *Mismeasure of Man*, or *Tristes Tropiques*. Often during the quarter, one faculty member will give a preparatory lecture before a book is discussed, but the main work of learning from the text and about the text, of making connections between the text and other parts of the program, occurs in the students' seminar discussions. Many faculty members find helping students develop rich, productive seminars the hardest work of the program but also the most rewarding.

In the book seminar for "The Basic Advantage" students discuss Sheila Tobias's *Succeed with Math*. At Seattle Central, faculty have linked the unlikely pair in "The Joy of Math and English" where students use their writing skills to help them understand and master mathematics. The math is taught in the regular sequence with emphasis on group work and board work; fundamental ideas such as equation as a whole sentence, word problem as stories, and mathematical solutions as narratives help ground a student's understanding. In the book seminar for this course, students read and discuss stories and plays that include mathematical concepts like August Wilson's *The Piano Lesson*.

Larger, Fully Integrated Programs or Coordinated Studies

If patterns of enrollment warrant it, a faculty team may propose a larger, fully integrated link—or coordinated studies—that amounts to the students' full course load and the faculty members' full teaching load. Faculty teams plan interdisciplinary programs for 60 to 80 students that may last a quarter or two, or a whole year. In the learning communities described earlier, faculty members may have two or more other teaching commitments, and the time given to the planning and tracking a learning community may seem an addition to the already heavy teaching load. Many community colleges offer the larger coordinated studies programs, and in these, faculty members find the most flexibility in establishing themes and developing schedules. In the last 15 years, Seattle Central has offered about 100 different, large team-taught interdisciplinary learning community programs, and courses from all disciplines have been integrated into them.

For the most part, the programs have been conceived as particularly interesting ways to deliver the curriculum, but they can serve many purposes. One program taught regularly by faculty from English, psychology, and biology is "Body and Mind," a one-quarter program designed for students who are going into health care programs or who want interesting ways to fulfill regular associates degree requirements. This program includes Zoology 113 (anatomy and physiology), a lab science, Psychology 110 (the standard introduction), and English 101. The grueling work of memorizing body parts is balanced by work in book seminars where students discuss essays by Lewis Thomas and novels by Doris Lessing and Mary Shelley. Thus, one learning community provides a supportive, nurturing entry program for students who will pursue a number of careers. The program helps them succeed with difficult prerequisites and builds community among the vocational students who will work together in upcoming quarters. At the same time, the program gives vocational students the opportunity to interact with students from the larger college population.

For all the students, the program is a stimulating and coherent learning experience.

Faculty teams may also organize programs in response to current issues. For instance, a team is now teaching "Africa in the Imagination." Posters advertising the course show several maps of Africa—including the Mercator and the Peters Projections. Underneath the maps is the question, "Which is the real Africa?" In this program students are encouraged to review critically images of Africa that they have absorbed and reproduced uncritically because of romantic films like *Out of Africa*, for instance. With faculty members using and introducing current textual strategies (based in part on influential post-structuralist works like Edward Said's *Orientalism*), students come to recognize distorted images of Africa and how they are constructed in texts. Students read about Africa in texts usually taught in different disciplines and written by Africans and by non-Africans. They consider the historical contexts in which the different Africas were constituted and the disciplinary assumptions, even discipline-based biases, which inform them. Thus, students read anthropological texts to understand the African cultures, while examining assumptions and methods an anthropologist brings to field work. Students learn to ask probing questions such as:

- What is the connection between myths governing books like Ernest Hemingway's *The Green Hills of Africa* and decisions made by the International Monetary Fund?

- What assumptions govern the study of a canonical text like Joseph Conrad's *Heart of Darkness*?

- What does it mean, at the end of the 20th century, to speak of African nations?

Despite early success of learning communities at Seattle Central, faculty noticed that African-American students were not registering for the courses. Several theories for their reluctance to participate were posited. Perhaps students saw learning communities as educationally fancy and impractical classes that might detour them from steady progress toward their goals. One faculty member noted that African-American students saw learning communities as "frills you could take if you were privileged" and didn't have to get on with serious schoolwork. In response, two faculty members designed "Our Ways of Knowing," a series of linked courses designed to meet the needs of African-American students. Disciplines typically include sociology, political science, anthropology, or English. These courses are not limited to African-American students, but African-Americans are targeted in recruitment efforts. Many African-American students have not been satisfied educationally because institutions do a kind of colonizing; if students do not do things in a certain way, they are on the outside. The aim of "Our Ways of Knowing," says one of its founders, "is to make these students insiders."

Because students often gravitate toward those whom they perceive to be connected to them culturally, the program, "Our Ways of Knowing," is taught primarily by African-American faculty. This connection is important in that faculty can make concepts clearer through shared cultural examples and language. Younger faculty may have an advantage because they are able to draw more readily on pop culture references. However, one faculty member indicates that what she wants is to "choreograph difference"; she discusses deviance and conformity using Mozart and bebop. These shared connections create a comfort zone in the college from which the students can bridge to other programs and courses. Faculty say they would like to see this program on the schedule every fall quarter, especially for entering African-American students. During subsequent quarters, then, the students will have the benefits of the network established in their first quarter. They may also feel encouraged to get off the beaten track in the future and take classes they may not have otherwise.

Other programs respond to the communities they

> Many African-American students have not been satisfied educationally because institutions do a kind of colonizing; if students do not do things in a certain way, they are on the outside. The aim of "Our Ways of Knowing," says one of its founders, "is to make these students insiders."

serve in other ways. A combination of courses that can be easily replicated is one like "A Billion Years of Washington History: Experiences in the Promised Land" (Northwest geology, anthropology of the Northwest, Washington State history, and freshman composition); these linked courses provide students with a deeper sense of the history of the region in which they live. Because the program comprises a students' whole schedule, the faculty members plan extended field trips to rock outcroppings, Hoover Dam, Hanford, archaeological digs, wilderness areas, and graveyards.

Vocational programs also gear themselves to the needs of the region. At Grays Harbor Community College near the estuary formed by the Chehalis River and the Pacific Ocean, learning communities are part of the Natural Resource Technology Program and respond directly to local environmental needs. In one of them, "Man, Machine, and Nature," taught by faculty in fisheries/natural resources, computer technology, and technical writing, students form an environmental consulting firm and complete a baseline survey of the college campus which includes a watershed. Based on their survey of natural resources—water, soil, trees—and on their development of a comprehensive recreation plan, the school received two different clean water grants (worth nearly $600,000) and built a model watershed. In the summer of 1997, Grays Harbor Community College held an institute supported by grant funding and organized as a learning community. The institute was designed to train high school and community college instructors in using learning communities to develop programs in natural resources. Participants report that they have used this experience to restructure the learning environments in their own classrooms.

Students make several trips to the desert while studying in "Journey to Ground Zero: Humans and the Desert," a ten-hour program at Solano College. The course begins with the proposition that the desert is a landscape that has shaped people and which people have shaped; students explore those relationships in writing and image making. They visit the Nevada Nuclear Testing Site as well as the Pinnacles National Monument, China Lake, and Death Valley.

Planning a fully integrated learning community may seem unsettling even if faculty members do not include week-long trips into the desert. After all those quarters, after all those years, experienced community college teachers know how to teach introductory courses in their disciplines. They have a syllabus—a sequence of topics, a selection of texts, the timing of artfully worded assignments, models for the midterm and final, essential points to be made in one or another already written lecture, afternoons for specific workshops, research trips, and films. All in all, the subject, whatever it is—politics in ancient Greece, introduction to sociology, or the literature of emerging nations—takes the shape of the syllabus, fitted to the teacher's special strengths. In learning communities, teachers must let go of that syllabus. Especially in fully integrated programs, the course content may appear in radically new contexts—different lights shine on it. Faculty members often prepare for teaching in links and coordinated studies by reading outside their fields and venturing out from what they know. Planning may feel like space travel: no gravity—some queasiness.

Faculty members, relying on each other, must proceed to reshape the curriculum with confidence in their disciplinary knowledge and pedagogical understanding. In a large, integrated learning community, the time and space limitations of the 50-minute classroom do not pertain. With an emphasis on collaborative teaching and learning, a learning community can include lectures, workshops, lab time, seminars, computer time and training, guest speakers, films, music, student presentations, peer editing, several kinds of group work and group assignments, exams, papers, portfolios, and self evaluations; it also may include some ten-hour days and extended field trips.

At the end of the quarter, students in the most unconventional integrated programs still receive credits for classes that industry or other educational institutions require. It remains the responsibility of each teacher to include within the learning community the required content of the course in his or her discipline. If credit is earned in Anthropology 120, English 102, History 230, or Biology 120, the fundamentals of those courses must be part of the program. Science faculty have discovered that "essential" is not necessarily everything in a 600-page textbook. Interdisciplinary teaching also encourages faculty to assess critically their disciplines, assumptions, and methods. As part of the planning procedure, a team of faculty defines essential knowledge in each discipline so that differences and similarities across disciplines are used dynamically—to set the key questions for the program and to structure classes around those questions.

Teaching and learning in learning communities invariably serves as a catalyst for instructors to rethink how they teach their regular courses and compels students to reform their ideas about school. From teaching and learning with students and colleagues, faculty members get new ideas about what can happen in a classroom—about books, technology, collaborative work, student-led seminars, exams, and writing assignments. They gain new expertise; a political scientist may assign Camus and a biologist *Ship Fever;* where a teacher simply may have lectured, he or she may now hold weekly seminars based on student research. Hundreds of faculty members who have had experience in learning communities are remodeling hundreds of free-standing introductory courses. Because so many community college students simply cannot afford the blocks of time required to take linked courses, the spill-over of learning community techniques into stand-alone classes may be the most telling effect of the learning communities initiative. Or, it may be the spill-over students report—that after a powerful experience in a learning community, their sense of what constitutes an education becomes so changed that they approach the rest of their college careers, however traditional, differently, enthusiastically. A student reports:

"When I decided to go back to school, I ended up in a coordinated studies program where I had an experience I never had before. The teacher left the lectern and sat beside me. Instead of having teachers just tell me what I should know, they were there learning with us, being exposed to subjects from new perspectives. That way each teacher also became a student. It wasn't such a power structure anymore, but a learning environment, humanized, where everyone was learning. I learned that I have knowledge, that I have what it takes to pursue knowledge, to gain knowledge. I left coordinated studies with the sense that I was free to learn rather than forced to learn."

In light of student responses like this one, some community colleges now require that students take one learning community course as part of the degree requirement.

Conclusion

Learning communities have a long history at Seattle Central. In the last 15 years, most faculty members in most divisions have taught in them, and new faculty members are encouraged to join colleagues in teaching one. Still, most classes are traditional: 50 minutes, one teacher. Directly and indirectly, however, the experiences of students and teachers in learning communities have changed the culture of education at Seattle Central Community College.

The student at my door was in a learning community, "Rediscovering the Americas," a few quarters ago. He tells me he has seen the Mayan ruins we read about, has improved his Spanish, is waiting tables to pay the rent, but just recently happened upon a few poems by Alexander Pope. Do I have the collected poems? I find a couple of different editions of Pope, and we head off to the

Atrium for the buffet luncheon prepared by the culinary arts students.

References

Astin, A. W. (1993). *What matters in college: Four critical years revisited.* San Francisco: Jossey-Bass.

Barrett, A. (1996). *Ship fever and other stories.* New York: Norton.

Conrad, J. (1929). Heart of darkness. *Youth and two other stories.* Garden City, NY: Doubleday.

Finley, N. J. (1990, Fall). Meeting expectations by making new connections: Curricular reform at Seattle Central. *Educational Record: The Magazine of Higher Education, 71*(4), 50-53.

Gould, S. J. (1981). *The mismeasure of man.* New York: Norton.

Hemingway, E. (1935). *The green hills of Africa.* New York: Scribner.

Levi-Strauss, C. (1974). *Tristes Tropiques.* (J. Weightman & D. Weightman, Trans.). New York: Atheneum.

Meiklejohn, A. (1932). *The experimental college.* New York: Harper & Row.

Said, E. (1979). *Orientalism.* New York: Vintage Books.

Tobias, S. (1987). *Succeed with math: Every student's guide to conquering math anxiety.* New York: Macmillan.

Wilson, A. (1990). *The piano lesson.* New York: Plume.

CHAPTER ELEVEN

Evaluating and Assessing Learning Communities

Kathi A. Ketcheson and Jodi H. Levine

The Latin derivation of assessment means "to sit beside" or "assist." In the modern world of higher education, assessment has taken on a variety of definitions and is often used interchangeably with "evaluation." Assessment is described as the systematic collection of information that can be used to describe student learning and can also be fed back to students, faculty, or administrators to strengthen or improve courses or programs. Assessment can take place on various levels: individual, classroom or group, program or discipline, and institution. If institutions are grouped into a system, then assessment can take place at that level as well. At each level, the focus is different. At the individual level, the focus is more clearly on students and student learning; on other levels, the focus broadens to other objectives, including accountability.

The National Science Foundation's *User-Friendly Handbook for Project Evaluation* defines evaluation as the "systematic investigation of the worth or merit of an object" (Stevens, Lawrenz, & Sharp, 1993, p. 1). Evaluation is conducted with a clear purpose that is usually action-related. The information collected should inform decisions about the program. In practice, evaluation should move beyond traditional notions of assessment as measurement and be considered in terms of how it can contribute to program development and success.

In this chapter, the terms "assessment" and "evaluation" are used interchangeably. Assessment is used to describe activities at the individual level, while evaluation is used to describe activities at the program level.

By adopting models of learning communities, colleges and universities have acknowledged that learning is not simply a linear process, with knowledge flowing in one direction from lecturer to students. In traditional models of education, tests, papers, and course grades serve as standard assessment tools in the classroom. Evaluations often are characterized by pretest/posttest designs that seek summative results about the course or program under study. Assessment of learning communities, however, requires a more creative approach which acknowledges that teaching and learning occur in a dynamic environment comprising various academic and social interactions. The purpose of this chapter is to share the experience of institutions involved in the assessment and evaluation of learning communities and to provide practical advice and guidance to those who are about to begin assessment or who need new ideas for ongoing assessment programs.

Designing and Managing Assessment of Learning Communities

Before embarking on a project, those involved in the assessment of learning communities should consider three questions: (a) Why are we doing this? (What is the purpose of the assessment?) (b) Who will be the subjects? and (c) What will be assessed? (Terenzini, 1994). The answers should be the product of open discussion, collaboration, and agreement among all groups and individuals who either will be involved in the assessment, or will be recipients of its results. Discussion of the "why" will include considerations of formative (process and improvement) or summative (accountability) purposes; the "who" will determine the level or levels at which assessment will occur, and the "what" will help shape the measures and techniques that will be used in the assessment.

Essential to assessment of learning communities is a well-stocked "toolbox," containing both qualitative and quantitative methods that can be used to examine the processes and outcomes of this approach to learning. Essential, too, is the understanding that interactions and exchanges occur at many levels—among faculty and students, faculty and other faculty, students and other students, students and staff, and among students as well as various individuals and activities in the environment external to the classroom or university. How is it possible to design assessments that consider all of these factors, and how is it possible to manage what could easily become an unmanageable process?

Most institutions involved in assessment would agree that the best piece of advice is to start small: Choose something that can be assessed using methods and resources immediately available and that will produce results within a reasonably short period of time. From this point, a broader research agenda can be developed. Assessment in complex environments such as learning communities can quickly become frustrating if measures are not taken to ensure that the process will be manageable right from the start. Planners should define goals and objectives up front and engage in dialogue with those who will be involved in the project to reach agreement not only over why, who, and what, but also over how the assessment should be conducted.

What Questions Should Be Asked?

There are many questions one can ask about how learning communities impact the freshman year experience. The challenge of shaping learning community evaluation and assessment activities is to define clearly the set of questions that can best inform your efforts. How do you know the program works? What information is needed to improve the program? How can assessment be carried out to convey information about the impact of the program on student learning, attitudes, and expectations?

Evaluation of learning communities involves two closely related agendas: proving and improving (MacGregor, 1995). Evaluation for proving involves recording and describing the impact of learning communities for both internal and external audiences, while evaluation for improving is conducted to gather information for the more internal purposes of problem solving and program enhancement. Coordination of these agendas must be at the center of planning an evaluation of learning communities.

Clearly stated goals and objectives are important components of any research design. Goals and desired outcomes defined at the beginning of the

> Essential to assessment of learning communities is a well-stocked "toolbox," containing both qualitative and quantitative methods that can be used to examine the processes and outcomes of this approach to learning.

project form important benchmarks in the evaluation of program progress and actual outcomes. Evaluation of the effectiveness of learning community programs, however, may reveal unintended or unexpected outcomes. Therefore, a flexible research design is essential to capture the broad picture of what students and teachers experience as members of learning communities. It is important to remember, however, that too much flexibility in a research design, or attempts to incorporate multiple research agendas, can defeat an evaluation effort before it gets underway.

The evaluation of learning communities includes multiple sources of information and multiple audiences. In addition, the information gathered often needs to be communicated to different audiences at different stages in program development. Examples of questions answered during the assessment process might include:

1. Who enrolls in learning communities?

2. Why do students choose to participate in learning communities?

3. How does participation in a learning community affect students' attitudes and expectations about the first year?

4. How does participation in a learning community affect students' academic performance in the first semester or first year? How does their performance compare to students who do not participate?

5. Do students who participate in learning communities stay in school longer and persist to graduation at higher rates than nonparticipants?

6. How does teaching a course as part of a learning community impact faculty attitudes about teaching and learning?

7. Do faculty teach differently when teaching as part of a learning community?

8. What is the context of the learning communities program within the institution?

Evaluation of learning communities is an ongoing process, and can become overwhelming if you do not plan and implement a regular schedule of evaluation and assessment activities. The questions asked during the implementation stage of the work will need to be repeated and reshaped as the program develops. As more students participate in and experience learning community programs, new questions will arise.

Know Your Students. Within learning communities, students are recognized not only as "learners," but also as "knowers" (Rendón, 1997). College campuses possess a diversity of students including traditional students, working students, returning adults, or those who may not be well-prepared for college. Many students bring with them a wealth of knowledge and experience gained through extracurricular activities, and these factors may confound attempts to attribute growth in student development solely to the educational experience. In designing assessment projects, it is important to have a portrait of the students in learning communities and a clear picture of the goals and objectives of the curriculum. Who are the students involved in the program? What are their backgrounds and characteristics, and how might these affect (a) the design of assessment projects, (b) how results are viewed, and (c) how results are interpreted?

What Methods Should Be Used?

In designing assessment, consideration must be given to the logic and thinking behind standard research design techniques, even when trying a new or alternate approach to assessment. These techniques provide a framework for the systematic collection and analysis of assessment information. A series of organized steps will help keep the process from becoming too complicated and unmanageable. A good, well-developed research design provides a map and compass for navigation over the complex, multidimensional terrain of learning communities.

Much of the information needed for evaluation and assessment exists in various forms on campus. Student records are available through admissions, registration, financial aid, or institutional research offices. These sources of information are often overlooked in favor of interviews or questionnaires, which may be subject to measurement error and bias. Many researchers argue strongly for "multiple and different measures of the same trait or behavior" (Terenzini, 1994). Wherever possible, information obtained from student records, records of student use of various services or facilities, or other archival sources with surveys, interviews, or observations of behavior can be combined and analyzed.

The term "multiple measures" is used frequently in assessment literature. In learning communities, a variety of activities typically take place in different settings, requiring a variety of tools. Surveys, individual interviews, focus groups, ethnography or field research, participant observation, classroom assessment techniques, student portfolios, self-assessment, or reflective journals are some tools appropriate to collecting assessment information in learning communities.

Early in the planning process, learning community organizers will need to take time to investigate the literature on research methods and to select data collection methods that are consistent with the kinds of questions being asked. Planners should also keep in mind that varying degrees of expertise are needed to use any of these tools, along with some knowledge of analysis and reporting techniques. It is important to do what is possible and appropriate to address the assessment questions and to present results that are understandable, usable, and accessible to all audiences.

Regardless of the approach or approaches you select, anticipation of and planning for sufficient resources—financial, human, and technical—are keys to ensuring success. For example, analysis of interview transcripts or open-ended survey questions takes a great deal of time but provides a rich source of assessment data that should not be neglected. A more efficient approach to assess-

ment will break the project down into smaller pieces and will include interviews along with other methods of data collection.

Questions of how data will be stored and maintained should be answered during the planning of assessment activities. Examples of these questions include: Who will have access to the information? Will it be used for purposes outside those of the assessment? Will students share in the results, and will they have input into how assessments are designed and used? What safeguards will be in place to protect the confidentiality of participants? If data are to be used for publications or presentations, compliance with research on human subjects guidelines may be necessary on your campus.

Collaborative Research. To streamline the evaluation process, those who assess learning communities will want to consider their needs and plans in the context of assessment activities already taking place on the campus. If the institution already collects and analyzes demographic data on entering students, this data may serve as a baseline for learning community research or be tailored to other assessment activities. Consultation with the unit or units responsible for institutional research may be helpful in shaping the learning community evaluation agenda. The consultation should also include a discussion of ways that the units can work together to meet both the institution and program's goals. These conversations may reveal that these goals are not mutually exclusive and that the information gathered in learning community assessment may inform other work at the institution.

There are many individuals on campus who can help gather, analyze, and interpret assessment data. They include faculty, students, student affairs professionals, and institutional researchers who are experienced in working with quantitative and qualitative information. The involvement of many individuals will supplement the

> To streamline the evaluation process, those who assess learning communities will want to consider their needs and plans in the context of assessment activities already taking place on the campus.

knowledge and expertise of the learning community staff while bringing a variety of perspectives to bear on the research. Broad campus participation in assessment activities increases the likelihood that results will be both accepted and used. In studies of three effective learning communities programs between 1992 and 1993, the research team of Goodsell Love, Russo, and Tinto (1995) concluded that the multiple methods/multiple researchers approach added richness and depth to their findings. They caution, however, that collaborative research requires close coordination in the initial stages and throughout the evaluation effort.

Faculty often have the best view of the multiple factors at work in the classroom. Classroom assessment is an effective way for teachers to discover how and what students are learning as the learning occurs. Angelo and Cross (1993) describe classroom assessment as "learner-centered, teacher-directed, mutually beneficial, formative, context-specific, ongoing, and firmly rooted in good practice" (p. 4). For example, the minute-paper exercise asks students to write down the most significant thing they learned in class and any remaining questions. This gives the instructor timely and directed feedback on what students learned or considered important for the day's lesson. It also allows instructors to make course adjustments as needed. Classroom assessment techniques can be used to improve the quality of student learning as well as the quality of teaching, both important outcomes for learning communities programs.

Discussions with students can reveal both intended and unintended outcomes of their participation in learning communities. Students can provide not only valuable insights into their learning experiences, but also how and when changes in learning and attitudes are likely to occur. In addition to information on the impact of learning communities, the assessment team is likely to collect valuable information on other aspects of students' freshman year experiences, ranging from the quality of academic advising to a review of dining center food.

As Terenzini notes (1994), research design involves a series of compromises. The choice of one approach may have implications for other parts of the project; what is desired may have to give way to what is possible given resource or time constraints. Careful identification of the purpose of a project and the audiences for which its results are intended must precede the development of a research design since these two factors shape the form and direction of a project (Goodsell Love, Russo, & Tinto, 1995).

What are the possible risks of not following a systematic approach to assessment of learning communities? The greatest risk may be that either too much or too little information will be collected or that the information gathered will not shed light on the research questions of interest. Another is the inability to interpret or use the stacks of surveys, interview transcripts, journals, or computer printouts resulting from the assessment. Some information may be interesting but may not be helpful in understanding the processes or outcomes that are the focus of the assessment. Many assessment efforts have been plagued by false starts. With careful planning and organization, these can be avoided. These steps may help in forming a process for the evaluation and assessment of learning communities:

1. Read the relevant literature.

2. Establish clear and measurable goals and objectives for the programs and courses you want to assess.

3. Develop a theoretical framework for assessments based on the theories of learning communities you have adopted on your campus.

4. Pose researchable questions, keeping in mind what is possible and appropriate to research.

5. Build in steps for reviewing the assessment process itself.

6. Identify the various audiences for your results.

7. Decide where you will go to get the information you need to answer your questions.

8. Conduct an inventory of existing data and data sources.

9. Choose data collection techniques that are practical and focused on your questions.

10. Choose appropriate analysis techniques, based on the types of data you have collected and what you want to know.

11. Decide what you will do with negative findings.

12. Report and disseminate results to your audiences using straightforward and understandable language, through accessible media.

13. Feed results back into programs or courses. Assessment should be linked to continuous improvement.

Using the Information

Research design should include a plan for how information gathered can be used to improve the program. What new knowledge about the program can be used to provide a better student experience in learning communities? In addition to demonstrating program effectiveness and impact, information on the experiences of first-year students in learning communities can be used to (a) increase student participation in the program, (b) broaden institutional support for the program and obtain additional resources, and (c) share examples of best practice with the higher education community.

If all students are not required to participate in learning communities, assessments should include information on who participates and why. Demographic information about participants will be important for future longitudinal studies on student performance and persistence. Interviews and focus groups with students can provide important information on why students choose to participate. Are they attracted to the program for the academic benefits, social benefits, or because of parental or peer influence?

It is also important to understand how students find out about learning communities. Effective recruitment and marketing strategies are crucial to the initial success of your program. Student feedback on the benefits of participation can be used to attract new students to the program and to increase campus support for the initiative.

Broadening institutional support for the program is essential in all phases of learning communities work: implementation, development, and maintenance of the effort. Rich and meaningful data on what students and faculty experience in learning communities can be used to demonstrate program impact on the first-year experience. Sharing all forms of evidence, even if it is anecdotal, with the general university community is one way to ensure the continuation of institutional support.

A frequently asked question is likely to be, "How does participation in a learning community impact student retention?" Program effectiveness can be measured by differences in retention rates for participants and nonparticipants or in terms of retention gains that can be causally related to learning communities. However, retention is only one piece of evidence that learning communities are an effective way to restructure the freshman year experience. Evaluation and assessment data should capture the full context of student experience—academic performance (grades, number of credits earned), persistence, perceptions, attitudes, and expectations.

The broader higher education community is an important audience for information on the impact of learning communities. As the number of campuses implementing learning communities increases, there is greater demand for evidence that learning communities work. National and regional conferences provide opportunities for campuses to come together to share examples of best practice and to discuss what worked and did not work in terms of the implementation of learning communities. A learning community e-mail discussion list maintained at Temple University provides another site to share this information.

(Instructions for subscribing to the discussion list are included at the end of Chapter 3.)

The information gathered on the learning community program needs to be interpreted and communicated to the decision makers, faculty, and students who can use the findings to maximize the benefits of participating in a learning community. Program leadership needs to discuss positive findings along with information on any areas in which the program needs improvement in order to achieve goals and desired outcomes. Evaluation should form the basis for recommendations to improve practice and avoid future problems.

Sharing Lessons Learned

The literature and experiences of colleagues point out the strengths and weaknesses of various approaches, the methodological issues inherent in the use of one tool or another, and the practical issues that arise when you attempt to analyze and interpret results. When developing the assessment plan, learning community staff should consider ways to build on or tailor the research designs and experiences of other campuses to the needs of their program. We conclude this chapter by sharing lessons from two institutions, Portland State University and Temple University, each of which took a very different approach to the evaluation of learning communities.

Lessons from Portland State University's University Studies Program

When Portland State University (PSU) initiated a comprehensive reform of the general education curriculum to a learning communities model in 1994, no university-wide assessment plan or experience was available to use as a guide. Staff and faculty associated with the program had to begin from scratch, reviewing literature, attending conferences and workshops, and experimenting with established techniques. The Offices of Institutional Research and Testing Services and faculty from across the university were brought together to design a framework and initial activities for the evaluation and assessment of the program. Faculty began experimenting with new teaching techniques, portfolios and journals, and classroom observers who could feed "real-time" assessment data directly back to the instructors.

Circumstances compelled the assessment team to ignore the advice to start small. This was due, in part, to initiatives underway at the state level to begin collection of system-wide assessment data. Work began with administration of a standardized assessment instrument given to all new first-year students as a pretest with the intent to administer the instrument again as a posttest during the senior year. The instrument was selected because it closely matched the goals of the curriculum. However, it was costly, lengthy, and involved complex recruitment, administration, and follow-up activities. Facing insufficient resources, underdeveloped research goals, and little faculty support, the activity disintegrated. In retrospect, the team noted that a lack of institutional history or experience with standardized assessment, combined with strong opposition from many faculty, had doomed the experiment from the beginning.

> In retrospect, the team noted that a lack of institutional history or experience with standardized assessment, combined with strong opposition from many faculty, had doomed the experiment from the beginning.

A second activity was more successful. The Classroom Environment Scales (CES), developed by Dr. Roger Winston and others (1989) at the University of Georgia has been used each year to capture students' impressions of the climate for learning in their first-year courses. Administered during winter term, the CES provides faculty with mid-year information on individual classes and the program as a whole. The instrument is administered and analyzed by the Office of Institutional Research and Planning (OIRP), which works with faculty teaching in the program to ensure that findings are presented in easily understood and usable formats.

One problem that the program assessment team did not gauge adequately was the sheer number of groups and individuals from other areas of the university who would seek assessment information on the program and its students during the first year. Initially, faculty believed that research on the program should be open to all. The result was that administration of various surveys, focus groups, and assessment tools was negotiated with individual faculty and students, with little or no coordination. In written comments on institutional surveys and in conversations with faculty and peers, students said that they felt like "guinea pigs" and resented being examined so closely. They also voiced their resistance to course-level and program-level assessments designed by faculty and administrators involved in the learning community. A delicate balance was struck between the freedom to conduct research and the integrity of teaching and learning in the program through establishment of a faculty council that worked to coordinate assessment activities and minimize the negative impact assessment was having on students.

With experience, the program assessment team discovered that standard assessment tools and techniques did not fit well with the style of teaching and learning that was evolving. It became apparent that these techniques were insufficient to capture changes in students' attitudes and academic development as they became involved in their own learning. Also, faculty found that their operationalization of program goals evolved over time as they and their students learned more about collaborative teaching and learning. Plans to coordinate and analyze data captured at the course level, through assignments and classroom experiences, resulted in three ongoing activities: (a) the formation of a faculty team to design a program-wide portfolio assessment rubric, (b) the development of an instrument to measure student learning goals during fall term and again during spring term of the first year, and (c) ethnographic study of one first-year course.

> The thinking behind assessment is moving away from "is what we are doing working?" toward "what have we done and what do we need yet to do?"

This information is complemented by a longitudinal project, initiated by the OIRP, that uses existing student records to track course-taking patterns, retention and attrition, and grades and combines this information with survey data collected through a panel of student and alumni surveys administered by OIRP. Reports of assessment activities conducted across all four years of the general education curriculum are drawn together in a comprehensive report used to identify what has been successful, what has not, and what is missing from the overall plan and distributed to the administration and campus community. The thinking behind assessment is moving away from "is what we are doing working?" toward "what have we done and what do we need yet to do?" This shift may lead to better integration of the general education curriculum with liberal studies and the majors and to a better understanding of what it means to be a graduate of PSU.

What did PSU learn from initial attempts to assess its learning community?

1. Assessment of learning communities requires time, resources, and the commitment of all participants. Ambitious projects may be difficult to implement without agreement among faculty, students, and administrators over the goals of the assessment and the uses for its results. Smaller assessment projects, set within an overall plan, may gain acceptance more readily and produce results for more immediate use by those involved. A well-defined set of goals and objectives must be established at the outset to help avoid the tendency to collect what is interesting but not necessarily useful or meaningful to anyone involved.

2. Many outcomes of learning communities may not be measurable using standard measurement techniques. The PSU experience suggested that experimentation with assessment techniques grounded in the classroom produced results that reflected modes of teaching and learning which occurred within the learning

community. Multiple methods of inquiry—bringing together surveys, portfolios, student self-reflection (essays, journals), interviews, in-class observations, and information from student records—are most effective.

3. Faculty, staff, and students must have an understanding of the need for and use of assessment data and agree to participate in assessment activities. Many of the difficulties experienced by PSU in using standardized assessments and program-wide surveys resulted from a lack of understanding and acceptance of the measures by students and faculty. Assessments developed in the classroom, and those on the program level into which faculty had input, were the easiest to administer and produced the most usable results.

4. Learning communities may be transforming while assessment is going on, requiring flexibility in the design and desired outcomes of assessment projects. Faculty at PSU found that definitions of goals, such as increased representation across geographical, ethnic, and racial barriers, continue to evolve as the learning community itself evolves. Although some agreement over how these goals can be measured has been achieved, everyone recognizes that these definitions may shift again as the program matures.

Lessons from the Evaluation of Temple University's Learning Communities Program

Temple University began its Learning Communities Program in 1993 on a grant from the Pew Charitable Trusts. The only assessment objective stipulated in the grant proposal was that Temple would monitor participants in terms of retention and achievement. During the initial stages, the program lacked a clearly defined plan to assess the impact of learning communities on the first cohorts of participants.

Initial assessment activities relied either on the usage of data already collected for other institutional purposes or on small-scale information-gathering techniques that did not require extensive human resources. The Offices of Student Information Systems and Measurement

and Research were able to provide the program with demographic data on students enrolled in communities. The Learning Communities Program conducted focus-group research that revealed useful information on what students expected and gained from participating in a community. Quotes from students were incorporated in literature designed to recruit entering students to learning communities and to describe the program to the general university community.

A study comparing grade point averages (GPAs) examined the impact of participation on student achievement. Annual comparison of GPAs revealed that learning communities participants received higher grades than nonparticipants in critical first-year courses such as college composition, college math, and general chemistry. One assessment activity conducted in the initial year of the program that was not productive was a survey mailed to participants and nonparticipants. Responses were not recorded or analyzed due to a low return rate, and to a lesser extent, a lack of sufficient human resources to handle data entry and analysis. The survey instrument, however, was later adapted for use in another survey project.

Focus-group research conducted in 1994 and 1995 proved to be an effective way to gather information about students' experiences as members of learning communities. Research reports were shared with program faculty and students, the university community, prospective students and their families, and other universities considering implementing learning communities. Grade analysis and demographic profiles also continued to be a part of ongoing assessment activities.

One initial problem the program encountered involved the design of a retention study. Before the study could be designed, system to identify and track program participants was needed. A system for coding participants by cohort year, beginning with Fall 1993 participants, was developed in conjunction with the Office of Student Information Systems. A second need was to define a representative group of nonparticipants for comparison. This task became increasingly difficult as participation in learning communities increased.

Ongoing conversations between the program and other offices involved in retention studies, however, resulted in an efficient design that annually produces meaningful retention information on participants and nonparticipants.

The major evaluation thrust came at the end of the grant period. The Learning Communities Program heeded the advice of the literature, and others in the field, and planned an evaluation that relied on a collaborative approach: multiple researchers relying on multiple methods of assessment. A not-for-profit research firm located in Philadelphia was brought in to conduct a qualitative case study focusing on the following questions: (a) How do people in different positions within the program (e.g., students, faculty) define the goals of learning communities? (b) How do students experience learning communities? (c) What characteristics of learning communities make a strong, positive experience for students? (d) How do professors and graduate assistants experience learning communities? and (e) What kind of connections does the Learning Communities Program have to the university as a whole?

The case study revealed that students spoke positively about their participation in a community. Students described ways learning communities enhanced their involvement in their courses and helped them connect with other students during the critical first semester. Faculty reported that teaching as part of a learning community influenced their pedagogy or attitude toward teaching and learning in some way. Interviews with colleagues across the university revealed that the learning communities program has a broad support base and that many individuals or offices feel that the program supports their work (Reumann-Moore, Haj, & Gold, 1997).

The Learning Communities Program conducted survey research to assess how participation in a community affected students' expectations and experiences in their first year at Temple. The Temple University Student Experience Survey, based in part on an instrument used in a national study of learning communities conducted by the National Center for Postsecondary Teaching, Learning, and Assessment (Tinto & Goodsell, 1993), was administered to a sample of participants and nonparticipants at three points in the academic year: the first two weeks of the fall semester, the end of the fall semester, and the end of the school year.

The survey captured meaningful information on how participation affected students' in- and out-of-class learning activities and their attitudes toward the university. Learning communities participants reported greater involvement with out-of-class learning activities, such as the formation of study groups. Learning communities students also reported greater satisfaction with the university environment.

Information gathered as part of the end-of-the grant evaluation, combined with data from the ongoing assessment activities (demographic, grade, and retention data), presented a picture of what students and faculty experience in learning communities. Findings were used to communicate the importance of learning communities in the freshman year to Temple students, faculty, and administration, as well as to prospective students. Findings also guided post-grant conversations about next steps for the program. What was going well and worthy of continuing? What work remains to improve the quality of academic life for Temple freshmen?

What did Temple learn from its initial attempts to assess learning communities?

1. Assessment of learning communities is an ongoing process that is best supported by a comprehensive evaluation plan outlined at the onset of the project. A more systematic evaluation plan helps program leadership stay a step ahead in terms of producing the information needed to demonstrate the impact of the program on students and faculty.

2. Lessons learned from assessment have multiple uses. Data gathered on what happens to students in learning communities became the focal point of recruitment activities. By telling students and faculty that learning community participants earned higher grades and stayed in school longer, and that students described

learning communities as "the best way to make the transition from high school to college," we were able to steadily increase student involvement, while simultaneously broadening support for the program across the university.

3. An evaluation of learning communities should include multiple researchers from within and outside the program. While use of external evaluators can be costly and in part takes assessment out of the hands of those most invested in the program, external evaluators add credibility to the findings. Collaboration between external and internal researchers can yield a thorough program evaluation that involves those most invested in the findings—the students and faculty participating in communities and the leadership guiding the effort.

Conclusion

Most definitions of assessment and evaluation include the notion of "systems"—assessment as a systematic collection of information and evaluation as a systematic investigation of a program's worth. As many chapters in this monograph stress, the work of learning communities is a systemic approach to improving teaching and learning at the undergraduate level, particularly for first-year students. This systems approach to building learning communities should be kept in place when it is time to assess and evaluate the project.

We began this chapter with a discussion of the Latin derivation of the term "assessment," and used this definition to stress the importance of assessment and evaluation in the planning process for learning communities. We end with the conclusion that the evaluation and assessment of learning communities do indeed "sit beside" the planning and implementation components of the work. Most texts describing program development place the evaluation chapter near or at the end of the text, and this monograph is no exception; however, decisions regarding assessment and evaluation should be made along side decisions about the design and development of learning communities.

References

Angelo, T. A., & Cross, K. P. (1993). *Classroom assessment techniques: A handbook for teachers* (2nd ed.). San Francisco: Jossey-Bass.

Goodsell Love, A., Russo, P., & Tinto, V. (1995). Assessment of collaborative learning programs: The promise of collaborative research. *Assessment in and of collaborative learning: A handbook of strategies.* Olympia, Washington: The Evergreen State College.

MacGregor, J. (1995). Going public: How collaborative learning and learning communities invite new assessment approaches. *Assessment in and of collaborative learning: A handbook of strategies.* Olympia, Washington: The Evergreen State College.

Rendón, L. I. (1997). *Unleashing the power of learning.* Keynote address at the Northwest Association of Special Programs, Region X. 17th Annual Fall Conference, Portland, Oregon.

Reumann-Moore, R., Abu El-Haj, T., & Gold, E. (1997). *Friends for school purposes: Learning communities and their role in building community at a large urban university.* Unpublished report, Temple University.

Stevens, F., Lawrenz, F., & Sharp, L. (1993). *User-friendly handbook for project evaluation: Science, mathematics, engineering and technology education.* Washington, DC: National Science Foundation.

Terenzini, P. T. (1994). The case for unobtrusive measures. In B. Townsend (Series ed.), J. S. Stark, & A. Thomas (Eds.), *Assessment and Evaluation,* (pp. 619-628). Needham Heights, Massachusetts: Simon and Schuster Custom Publishing.

Tinto, V., & Goodsell, A. (1993) *A longitudinal study of freshman interest groups at The University of Washington.* University Park, Pennsylvania: Pennsylvania State University, The National Center on Postsecond-ary Teaching, Learning and Assessment.

Winston, R. B., Vahala, M. B., Gillis, M. F., & Nichols, E. C. (1989). *College classroom environment scales*. (Form 8.89). Athens, Georgia: University of Georgia.

CHAPTER TWELVE
Trends and Future Directions

John N. Gardner and Jodi H. Levine

As we indicated in our opening statements to this monograph, our intent herein was to explore the pedagogical and structural innovations taking place on college campuses as a result of learning communities. The first chapter defined the concept of learning communities and provided an overview and historical perspective of this movement in higher education. Subsequent chapters highlighted learning community models at institutions across the country and examined the resources necessary to sustain learning communities and the challenges to their success. In this, the concluding, chapter, we identify and summarize the major ideas and issues that frame learning community work. Based on the models presented and issues discussed elsewhere in this monograph, we present a series of recommendations for educators who are developing or working in learning communities.

Conversations about student learning are occurring simultaneously on multiple levels: within individual classrooms, across campuses, in state legislatures, and in national forums on higher education. Peter Ewell (1997) asks us to consider undergraduate reform in the context of what we know about promoting learning and managing institutional change; for example, settings that emphasize interpersonal collaboration promote learning. He cites cross-curricular learning communities as an effective practice that helps students and faculty form partnerships for learning. Ewell (1997) also describes the type of change needed for institutions to reorganize for learning. "Change requires people to relearn their roles" (p. 6). As this monograph repeatedly demonstrates, learning communities recognize not only that students and faculty are central to the learning process, but also that academic advisers, residence life staff, and other campus professionals must be included in efforts to promote learning.

One of the overarching beliefs present in this monograph is that learning communities are an effective approach to transforming the teaching and learning culture on college campuses. Learning communities are effective in this capacity for the following reasons:

1. Designing learning communities provides an opportunity to examine general education requirements and how students experience general education

courses. Many campuses install learning communities as part of general education reform, while others use learning communities as a way to improve teaching, learning, and student satisfaction with general education. Learning communities also serve to integrate otherwise unconnected general education courses, especially in the first year.

2. Learning communities foster conversations between faculty on how and when learning occurs in their classrooms. When faculty offer their courses as part of learning communities, these conversations take on deeper meaning as faculty consider ways of integrating their courses.

3. Participation in learning communities asks that students take a more active role in their own learning. Examination of learning community classrooms reveals that students are asking questions and participating in discussions more frequently. Students are more comfortable working in groups and are more likely to recognize their classmates as a resource.

4. Attending classes with linkages that bring more meaning to courses allows students to begin to see the connections between history, philosophy, and writing, or between mathematics and psychology.

5. Building learning communities and examining what happens to students and faculty who form communities increases campus awareness that learning occurs both in and out of the classroom. Academic advisers, student affairs professionals, residence life staff, and peer leaders play a critical role in developing the curricular and co-curricular dimensions of learning communities. Thus learning communities provide an ideal vehicle for improved academic/student affairs partnerships.

6. Learning communities give campuses a critical lens through which to examine the teaching and learning culture, providing us with possible answers to critical questions: (a) At what levels are students achieving? (b) How do students evaluate their general education courses? (c) How can we better support student learning?

7. Learning community classrooms invite alternate modes of assessing teaching and learning. Classroom research and assessment are effective techniques to document what happens to students and teachers in learning communities.

8. Learning communities send prospective and entering students the message that "how you learn" is as valued as "what you learn." Campuses committed to learning communities, particularly for first-year students, communicate an important message that they are truly committed to first-year students' learning, success, satisfaction, and retention, and that they are therefore willing to challenge traditional models of teaching and learning. On these campuses, new students are less likely to find themselves as passive learners in large lecture sections.

What We Have Learned from this Monograph

1. Meaningful change in higher education requires cross-campus collaboration. Every learning community example described in this monograph mentions some level of collaboration that was necessary to realize learning communities.

2. Implementing learning communities requires a strong degree of academic risk taking. Learning community models challenge traditional values in higher education (especially that of the individual faculty member dispensing knowledge from an isolated lectern, unconnected to the courses and teaching of colleagues).

To develop the cross-campus partnerships needed to make learning communities thrive, campuses need to identify and articulate goals that warrant an overall commitment, such as improved retention, greater satisfaction with the college experience, and greater tolerance for diversity.

Learning communities ask faculty and students to teach and learn in ways that at first might feel daunting and uncomfortable.

3. To address increasing demands for accountability, campuses are looking for innovative ways to improve student performance and persistence. As more evidence of the success of learning communities is shared with the higher education community, more campuses will consider learning communities as part of their efforts to improve teaching and learning at the undergraduate level.

4. To improve retention, and even to increase new student enrollment, campuses are front-loading resources into the critical first year. The growth of first-year seminars and learning communities (preferably combined and integrated so they reinforce each other's positive impact) across the country is evidence that colleges and universities recognize the importance of the first-year experience to undergraduate satisfaction and success.

5. The learning community is an approach to undergraduate reform that can be adapted to any campus setting. This monograph includes examples of successful learning communities on community college, residential, commuter, urban, and suburban campuses.

6. Goals for learning communities are often conceived in a broader context than the program level. To develop the cross-campus partnerships needed to make learning communities thrive, campuses need to identify and articulate goals that warrant an overall commitment, such as improved retention, greater satisfaction with the college experience, and greater tolerance for diversity.

Central Themes and Issues

Learning communities assume a variety of forms; however, certain central themes, characteristics, and issues emerge regarding their overall traits, organization, teaching, and implementation on specific campuses, especially two-year institutions. Our overview of these central themes and issues draws heavily on the evidence and practical models presented elsewhere in this monograph.

Overall Traits of Learning Communities

As Gabelnick, MacGregor, Matthews, and Smith (1990) state, "Learning communities are attractive because they address in a myriad of ways issues of curricular coherence, civic leadership, student retention, active learning, educational reform, and faculty development" (p. 10). Their flexibility and adaptability to various campus settings make them highly successful structures for achieving student and faculty collaboration, unifying the curriculum into a coherent whole, and creating interactive pedagogies.

Traditional college courses are often limited and defined by the institutions preferred scheduling plan. While some learning community models work within this standard schedule, team-taught programs create their own schedules. Block scheduling in team-taught programs allows topics to be covered in greater depth and does not arbitrarily cut off student learning and inquiry because the 50 minutes are up.

While learning communities are often geared toward special populations such as first-year students, underprepared students, and minority students, no evidence exists to suggest that learning communities work better for these special target groups than they do for any other student groups. On the contrary, research suggests that the shared learning between students and faculty that occurs in learning communities can be beneficial to all types of students. Because learning communities are uniquely able to capitalize on the development of the student peer group, they are especially effective tools for shaping student learning.

Organization of and Resources for Learning Communities

Learning communities are generally non-discipline specific, can involve any number of departments and faculty members, and can be offered for any student population. Although there are many possible structures and administrative homes, every learning community needs a coordinator—often a faculty member—or an administrator who will advocate for the needs of the learning community. Ideally, the coordinator works with an advisory committee that represents all stakeholders, including students, who have an investment in learning communities.

It is understood that resources must be provided for the implementation of a successful learning community. Some programs, like the Learning Communities Program at Temple University, are started with resources from external funding sources and then rely on university resources for future growth and development. Other programs (such as the FIG program at the University of Missouri-Columbia) are supported by funding from both academic and student affairs units.

Teaching and Faculty Development in the Learning Community

Teaching in a learning community is, for many faculty, a new and different experience as it redefines traditional relationships among faculty, students, and departments. Therefore, faculty development activities are especially critical. Faculty report that such activities can be transformative, resulting in increased collegiality, a renewed focus on student learning, and increased knowledge and use of campus resources. Additionally, learning communities often involve additional work for faculty; development opportunities are a welcome source of compensation when "real dollars" are scarce.

Learning Communities in the Two-Year College

Learning communities can be and have been successful in every type of campus setting. But considering the fact that more than 50% of America's first-year students are enrolled in community colleges, we found it highly appropriate to emphasize in a separate monograph chapter the current types of learning communities which are found in community colleges. Learning communities are a vehicle for putting the "community" in the community college because they offer a cohesive, integrating element in a campus culture whose highly diverse, transient, and non-residential student body creates fragmentation. In many ways, learning communities in the community college are on the cutting edge. A whole spectrum of approaches to learning communities has been implemented in the community college setting: linked courses, fully integrated links featuring block scheduling and team teaching, and coordinated studies programs that comprise the student and faculty member's entire course load. In community colleges, the success of learning communities serves as encouragement to and demonstration for faculty in baccalaureate-level institutions. If this concept can be implemented in the community college, then we should be less tolerant of arguments that this notion cannot work in the baccalaureate sector.

Final Recommendations

The strength of this monograph is that it is grounded in practical examples provided by faculty and student affairs administrators who have planned, implemented, and worked in learning communities on their own campuses. We close this chapter and this monograph by offering a list of recommendations which we have gleaned from the preceding chapters and from our own work in administering a variety of higher education programs, both in and out of the classroom.

1. Several approaches to learning communities are discussed in this monograph. Just as there is no ultimate definition of "learning community," there is no best approach to the work. We recommend that those involved in learning communities carefully consider the goals of the project and select the model best suited to the teaching and learning environment of the campus. We also recommend a heightened awareness of how the faculty, student, and student affairs cultures intersect and interact so that learning communities can be developed out of a *campus* awareness of what it takes to promote student success.

2. The effectiveness of learning communities, and the success of first-year students especially, can be enhanced by incorporating a variety of components into the learning community format and context such as: orientation, advising,

peer mentoring, peer advising. These components stress elements of social, emotional, and cognitive development vitally important for new students.

3. Because of the inherent administrative challenges, we recommend that institutions begin a learning community program with a limited number of sections. After evaluating those pilot sections, the program can be gradually expanded.

4. Learning communities can provide an opportunity for the development of intentional partnerships between academic and student affairs. We recommend the creation of seamless learning environments that capitalize on the interrelatedness of the in- and out-of-class influences on student learning, helping students reach their maximum potential. Yet the seamless learning environment cannot be created unless the obvious differences between academic and student affairs objectives, functions, roles, and cultures are overcome. Senior administrators and academic and student affairs must be strong champions and advocates for innovation and change and must make visible their commitments to developing, nurturing, and sustaining such partnerships.

5. We recommend the combining of learning communities with other retention initiatives (e.g., first-year seminars and living/learning structures within residence halls) so as to increase the probability of greater impact on students. Learning communities have also been found highly effective vehicles for delivery of academic advising and other support programs when these processes are integrated into a credit-bearing, new student seminar course.

6. We recommend that institutions launching a learning community provide appropriate faculty development support for the design, initiation, and ongoing development. It would be unwise to allow faculty to teach in learning communities without devoting the extensive time, energy, and efforts necessary to think through the essential design implications of collaborative learning. In order to achieve the full

potential of increased student learning and academic performance, faculty must receive training that will help them step outside the box of traditional classroom pedagogy.

7. We recommend providing several settings for those involved in learning communities to debrief and talk about their participation. Throughout this monograph we have described learning communities as a change process. Building and sustaining learning communities challenge traditional models of teaching and learning and require cooperation between units not normally accustomed to working together. Learning community planners, faculty, and students need to share their experiences--the small victories and triumphs along with the trials and tribulations.

8. Ongoing assessment is crucial to the success of learning communities. We recommend including an assessment plan in the early stages of program development and identifying ways to feed the findings back into the program. In launching assessment of the learning community, three important initial questions must be answered: (a) Why are we doing this (i.e., what is the purpose of the assessment)? (b) Who will be the subjects? and (c) What will be assessed? (Terenzini, 1994).

9. To enhance the credibility of assessment results, we recommend that the assessment of learning communities be performed by some individual(s) who have no responsibility for the administration and the design of these programs and who are perceived by members of the campus community as researchers with both high integrity and outstanding credentials.

10. We recommend that initial assessment efforts focus on something that can be measured using methods and resources immediately available and that will produce results within a reasonably short period of time. These initial assessment efforts can be used to develop a broader and more complex research agenda.

11. We recommend using both quantitative and qualitative methodologies in the assessment of

learning communities. A variety of techniques should be used including surveys, individual interviews, focus groups, ethnography or field research, participant observation, classroom assessment techniques, student portfolios, self-assessment by students and faculty, and reflective student writing. Assessment also provides an excellent opportunity for collaboration between many different sectors of the campus all of which have a stake in learning community student success (faculty, academic administrators, student affairs officers, institutional researchers, planners, and policy makers).

12 . Finally, while all of us are interested in enhancing student retention, we should be careful about viewing this as the determining factor in whether learning communities "work." Retention is only one piece of evidence that learning communities are an effective way to restructure the first-year experience to enhance learning, promote student and faculty development. Assessment must capture the full context of student, faculty, and staff experiences of learning communities: academic performance, persistence, perceptions, attitudes, and outcomes versus expectations. It is extremely important to involve faculty in all stages of the design, implementation, interpretation, and dissemination of assessment findings. Assessment must not be something "imposed" on unwilling or uninformed faculty and student participants.

Higher education is facing increasing demands for accountability from both internal and external constituencies. We are asked not only to provide evidence of what students are learning but also to document that they are learning in more meaningful ways, ways that will help them graduate better prepared for the workplace of the 21st century.

References

Ewell, P. T. (1997). Organizing for learning: A point of entry. *National Center for Higher Education—Management Systems (NCHEMS)*. Draft prepared for discussion at the American Association for Higher Education Summer Academy at Snowbird.

Gabelnick, F., MacGregor, J., Matthews, R. S., & Smith, B. L. (1990). Learning communities: Creating connections among students, faculty, and disciplines. *New Directions for Teaching and Learning, 41.* San Francisco: Jossey-Bass.

Terenzini, P. T. (1994). The case for unobtrusive measures. In B. Townsend (Series Ed.), J. S. Stark, & A. Thomas (Eds.), *Assessment and evaluation,* (pp. 619-628). Needham Heights, MA: Simon and Schuster.

About The Authors

Betsy O. Barefoot is Co-Director for Research and Publications in the National Resource Center for The First-Year Experience and Students in Transition at the University of South Carolina. She serves as editor or co-editor for all Center publications and has authored several publications and monographs on the first-year experience. Barefoot is a clinical faculty member in the University's College of Education where she teaches graduate courses in higher education administration. She received her B.A. (1976) degree from Duke University and her M.Ed. (1987) and Ed.D. (1992) degrees from the College of William and Mary.

Jack W. Bennett earned his B.A. and Ph.D. (in English) from the University of Oregon, where he now is an Associate Professor and director of the Freshman Interest Group (FIG) program. He has co-authored a book, *Applying to Graduate School*, and he launched the first FIG program in the nation in 1982. Bennett has consulted with universities in the USA, Canada, and Australia about developing FIG programs. Besides regularly teaching literature courses and directing the FIG program, he is interested in advising issues with undeclared students and prelaw students.

Valerie A. Bystrom has taught at Seattle Central Community College since 1970. She did both undergraduate and graduate work in English literature at the University of Washington in the 1960s and finished her Ph.D. in 1974. In 1984 she was asked to join two other teachers and sixty students in a learning community at The Evergreen State College; subsequently, she helped launch coordinated studies programs at Seattle Central. She is a founding member of the Washington Center for Improving the Quality of Undergraduate Education.

Emily Decker is Associate Director of the Washington Center for Improving the Quality of Undergraduate Education at The Evergreen State College. Decker's educational background includes a B.A. in English literature from Augustana College and an M.A. and a Ph.D. in English from the University of Michigan. Prior to her work with the Washington Center, Decker taught a variety of writing courses in the English Composition Board at the University of Michigan. She also directed the design and implementation of a campus-wide portfolio-based assessment of undergraduate student writing at the University of Michigan.

Jeanine L. Elliott is Director of the Washington Center for Improving the Quality of Undergraduate Education at The Evergreen State College. The Washington Center, a consortium of 46 two-year and four-year colleges and universities in Washington state, focuses on learning communities, collaborative learning, cultural pluralism, academic success of students of color, reform calculus, introductory, interdisciplinary science, and technology on a human scale. Elliott's educational background includes an undergraduate degree in English literature from the University of Illinois, theological training at Chicago Theological Seminary and the University of Chicago, and a Ph.D. from The Union Institute in Women's Studies and Higher Education.

Kenneth K. Etzkorn is Director of Curriculum Planning and Special Programs in the Office of Undergraduate Education at the University of Washington and has served as co-director of UW's Freshman Interest Group program since 1995. He also serves as a member of UWired, a campus-wide technology initiative and is involved with several groups working on issues of accountability in education. Prior to his current position, Etzkorn directed the general studies program and served as an academic counselor, working primarily with new students and students unsure of their major.

Scott E. Evenbeck earned a B.A. in psychology from Indiana University and an M.A. and Ph.D. in social psychology from the University of North Carolina at Chapel Hill. Currently, he is an Associate Professor of Psychology at Indiana University Purdue University Indianapolis (IUPUI). He has served in several administrative positions including Associate Dean of the Faculties and Director of Continuing Studies at IUPUI. He has also served as a member of an instructional team for a learning community course geared toward first-year students. Evenbeck is currently Dean of the University College.

Dorothy S. Fidler is the Senior Managing Editor at the National Resource Center for The First-Year Experience and Students in Transition at the University of South Carolina (USC). She received her B.A. (1959) from Duke University and Ph.D. (1980) in Experimental Psychology from the University of South Carolina. In 1987 she helped establish the National Resource Center. Fidler teaches courses in psychology, women's studies, and special sections of University 101 for adult students. She also serves as an academic advisor to adult students.

John N. Gardner is founder and Director of the National Resource Center for The First-Year Experience and Students in Transition at the University of South Carolina. Gardner is the nation's most recognized advocate for first-year students and was selected by the American Association for Higher Education as one of 20 faculty in the United States for "outstanding leadership contributions to their institutions and/or American higher education." Gardner received his B.A. (1965) degree from Marietta College, his M.A. (1967) from Purdue University, and honorary doctorates from Marietta College, Baldwin Wallace College, and Bridgewater State College.

Barbara Jackson is an Associate Professor of Anthropology at Indiana University Purdue University Indianapolis (IUPUI). She received her doctoral degree from the University of Minnesota. Jackson teaches gender in cross-cultural perspective and ethnographic research methods and has also served as a member of the instructional team for a learning community geared toward first-year students at IUPUI. Her administrative responsibilities center on faculty and curriculum development. She is currently serving as Associate Dean of the University College.

Jason N. Johnson is the Assistant Director of New Student Programs at the University of Washington, Seattle. He received a B.A. in Comparative History of Ideas from the University of Washington in 1997 and is currently working toward a M.Ed. in Higher Education Leadership and Policy Studies. Johnson was a Freshman Interest Group peer instructor for two years as an undergraduate, and has coordinated the FIG program with Michaelann Jundt and Ken Etzkorn since 1996.

Michaelann M. Jundt is the Director of New Student Programs at the University of Washington. She and her staff coordinate Freshman Interest

Groups, Transfer and Returning Student Interest Groups, Freshman Seminars, and orientation programs for new students and their families. Jundt is also involved in a campus-wide technology initiative called UWired. She is on the Planning Committee for the Washington Center and has been involved with the National Orientation Directors Association, Mortar Board, and several national learning community groups.

Kathi A. Ketcheson, a native of the Pacific Northwest, received her B.A. (1979) in History from the University of Washington and her M.S. (1983) in Public Administration and Ph.D. (1996) in Urban Studies from Portland State University (PSU). She has facilitated sessions and presented workshops and papers on institutional research and assessment at both regional and national conferences. Currently, Ketcheson serves as Director of Institutional Research and Planning at PSU where she is involved in a variety of activities including student and alumni surveys, assessment, curricular reform, budgets and planning, and the implementation of performance indicators.

Jodi H. Levine is Director of First-Year Programs at Temple University. In this role, she directs the University's learning communities, freshman seminar, and Supplemental Instruction initiatives. She received her B.A. (1988) in Political Science and her M.S. in Higher Education (1989) from Syracuse University. In 1995, she received her Ed.D. in Educational Administration from Temple University. Levine has published and presented on various issues related to designing, implementing, sustaining, and evaluating learning communities. She is co-authoring an upcoming Jossey-Bass publication, *Creating Learning Communities.*

Anne Goodsell Love is Assistant Dean of University College at the University of Akron, overseeing the University Orientation 101 course, learning communities for first-year students, and new student orientation programs. Dr. Love received a Ph.D. in Higher Education from Syracuse University, an M.Ed. in Counselor Education from The Pennsylvania State University, and a B.S. in Psychology from St. Lawrence University. She is co-author of *Enhancing Student Learning: Intellectual, Social, and Emotional Integration,* and editor of *Collaborative Learning: A Sourcebook for Higher Education.* She has written numerous articles about learning communities and is a Consulting Editor for the ASHE-ERIC Higher Education Report Series.

John McGrew is an Associate Professor of Psychology at Indiana University Purdue University Indianapolis (IUPUI). He received his doctoral degree from Indiana University at Bloomington. He teaches in the undergraduate psychology program and in the clinical rehabilitation psychology Ph.D. program. McGrew has also served as a member of the instructional team for a learning community geared toward first-year students at IUPUI. He is the author of over 25 book chapters and articles in the area of psychiatric rehabilitation.

Frankie D. Minor is the Director of Residential Life at the University of Missouri-Columbia. He has served as the chief housing officer at Saint Louis University and Saint Leo College during his 15 years in higher education. Minor received his M.A. from Bowling Green State University and B.A. from the University of Florida. Active in the American College Personnel Association and Association of College and University Housing Officers - International, he has presented and written on areas of community development, student involvement, and most recently on the creation of learning communities and other integrated learning experiences.

Philip S. Moore currently serves as the Director of Assessment and Associate Director of Institutional Planning and Assessment at the University of South Carolina. His current research interests include assessing student outcomes and creating a data warehouse and web applications for institutional research. He received his Ph.D. in Educational Psychology and Research from the University of South Carolina.

Melissa R. Roberts received her B.S. (1996) in psychology from Francis Marion University and her M.Ed. (1998) in Student Personnel Services from the University of South Carolina. As a graduate student at USC, she worked with the Director of Student Life and served as an intern in the National Resource Center for The First-Year Experience and Students in Transition.

Charles C. Schroeder received his B.A. and M.A. degrees from Austin College and his doctorate (1972) from Oregon State University. During the past 17 years, he has served as the chief student affairs officer at Mercer University, Saint Louis University, Georgia Institute of Technology, and University of Missouri-Columbia. He has assumed various leadership roles in the American College Personnel Association, serving as President in 1986 and 1993. Schroeder has published over 30 articles and published a book in 1994 with Phyllis Mable entitled *Realizing the Educational Potential of Residence Halls.*

Diane W. Strommer is currently the Dean of Zayed University in the United Arab Emirates. She is co-author of *Teaching College Freshmen*, published by Jossey-Bass in 1991. She is also the author of three other books and numerous articles. While serving as Dean of University College at the University of Rhode Island, she established the Feinstein Center for Service Learning, a Learning Assistance Center, and the Office of International Education. Dr. Strommer earned her B.A. in English literature at the University of North Carolina, Chapel Hill, and her M.A. and Ph.D. degrees, also in English literature, from The Ohio State University.

Theodore A. Tarkow received his A.B. in classics from Oberlin College and his M.A. and Ph.D. in Classics from the University of Michigan. He joined the faculty of the University of Missouri-Columbia in 1970, and is presently Professor of Classical Studies and Associate Dean of Arts and Science, a position he has held since 1982. As Associate Dean of Arts and Science, he has worked to initiate a variety of projects to strengthen the quality of undergraduate education in Missouri-Columbia's largest and most diverse undergraduate division.

Kenneth A. Tokuno is Dean of Student Services at Leeward Community College in Pearl City, Hawaii. He received an A.A. from American River College in 1967, a B.S. (Biochemistry, 1969) and an M.S. (Child Development, 1973) from the University of California at Davis, and a Ph.D. in Developmental Psychology from the University of Hawaii at Manoa in 1977. Tokuno has been an assistant professor of Human Development at the University of Hawaii at Manoa and an academic counselor and Director of Curriculum and Programs at the University of Washington (UW). He helped found and develop the Freshman Interest Group program at UW.